George Montague Wheeler

Lt. George M. Wheeler, U.S. Army Corps of Engineers.

During Wheeler's conduct of the reconnaissances and surveys west of the one-hundredth meridian from 1869 to 1879, much of historical importance happened that he did not wish to make public. Gradually, historians are separating the myth from the man.

Photo courtesy of Arizona and the West *and National Archives*

GEORGE MONTAGUE WHEELER

The Man and The Myth

Doris Ostrander Dawdy

SWALLOW PRESS/OHIO UNIVERSITY PRESS

ATHENS

Swallow Press/Ohio University Press books are printed on acid-free paper ∞

97 96 95 94 93 5 4 3 2 1

Library of Congress Cataloging-in-Publication

Dawdy, Doris Ostrander.
George Montague Wheeler : the man and the myth / Doris Ostrander Dawdy.
p. cm.
Includes bibliographical references and index.
ISBN 0-8040-0973-2
1. Wheeler, George M. (George Montague), 1842–1905. 2. Explorers—Southwest, New—Biography. 3. Southwest, New—Discovery and exploration. 4. United States—Exploring expeditions. 5. West (U.S.)—Description and travel—1860–1880. I. Title.
F786.W55D38 1993
917.904′2′092—dc20
[B] 93-12998
CIP

Contents

Acknowledgments

The Wheeler story required a great deal of detective work that would not have been accomplished without the assistance of archivists, librarians, and editors specializing in Western Americana. In 1976, John Irwin, special collections archivist at Northern Arizona University, showed me the journal of one of Wheeler's artists which he had been instrumental in acquiring for the university. While researching and writing the first volume of *Artists of the American West* I had often wondered what expedition Alexander H. Wyant had joined in 1873 and so I instantly sought permission for use of the journal. Irwin generously granted me exclusive use for a three-year period. My progress in producing a work fit for publication was slow, necessitating a six-month extension which was granted by Irwin's successor, archivist William Mullane. Without their cooperation and without the editing expertise of historian Harwood P. Hinton who assisted me in preparing the journal for publication in *Arizona and the West,* neither the journal nor this book was likely to see print. Wyant's journal with my annotations was published in the Autumn 1980 issue. At that time I was completing the first draft of *George Montague Wheeler: The Man and the Myth.* In 1986, shortly before Dr. Hinton resigned his editorship of *Arizona and the West,* he granted permission for further use of the annotated journal, in whole or in part, for this book.

At the National Archives in Washington, D.C., where I did most of the research on Wheeler, archivists Sara Jackson, Stuart Butler, Michael Musick, and John Dwyer were especially helpful. Military historians who became interested in my research and were helpful include William Gardner Bell, Paul Scheips, and Frank Schubert. The last loaned me his research notes for the book he was writing on the exploration and mapping of the West by the army's Topographical Corps, which included information developed by geologist Peter Guth, a West Point graduate whose dissertation was on Wheeler.

Through archivist Stuart Butler I met Dennis Casebier, author of *Tales of the Mojave Road,* who was doing research at the National Archives for a seventh book in that series. He kindly shared his information on Wheeler's mining properties in Mohave County, Arizona. At my suggestion Casebier and I met with Guth to discuss our mutual interest in George Montague Wheeler and to share information.

At the U.S. Geological Survey library in Reston, Virginia, where I had gone to study the maps of the four principal leaders of the western surveys, I met paleontologist Clifford Nelson, then serving as associate historian. Occasionally Nelson found time to talk about those surveys and to show me records and drawings not available in other archival holdings.

Following my return to California in 1981, I went through a series of drafts of the Wheeler book which were not improving with time. Historian C. L. Sonnichsen, then editor of *Arizona Historical Society Journal,* got me out of that rut when I wrote him of my dilemma. A beloved professor by those who studied under him, and honored by those like myself who knew him through his writings, Sonnichsen will be long remembered for his assistance to writers intent upon becoming published authors. Not only did he read one draft, but a second draft that I had revised in accordance with his suggestions.

Others who have been especially helpful and supportive include historian Dwight L. Smith, who has contributed various articles and books to my library, including his own published works on subjects related to the Wheeler survey; author Constance Wynn Alshuler, who specializes in military research and shared her information on Wheeler; media specialist Barbara Dahl, who read an early draft; and my husband David R. Dawdy, who shares interest in western history and rescues me when the word processor goes awry.

Librarians deserve a special word of appreciation. The information I needed was not easy to locate and necessitated my going to many public and specialized libraries. In California I used the California State Library in Sacramento and its Sutro branch in San Francisco, the San Francisco Public Library, the San Francisco State University library, the University of California libraries in Berkeley and Irvine, the Corps of Engineers' San Francisco library, and the U.S. Geological Survey library in Menlo Park. In Colorado I used the Denver Public Library's western history collection and the University of Colorado's special collection library. In Arizona, I used the university library in Tucson, and in Nevada, I used the university library in Reno and the state library in Carson City. Librarians at these institutions made my hours of research pleasant and productive.

Introduction

This treatment of Lt. George Montague Wheeler and his surveys west of the one hundredth meridian confronts the inaccuracies in his annual and final reports, published from 1870 to 1889, and exposes a hidden agenda not previously considered by historians. In the service of the U.S. Army Corps of Engineers from 1866 until he retired in 1888, Wheeler headed the War Department's mapping program authorized by Congress upon passage of the act of June 10, 1872.

In March 1879 came the legislative blow that consolidated the western surveys of Wheeler, Ferdinand Vandeveer Hayden, Clarence King, and John Wesley Powell and assigned their functions to the Interior Department. Wheeler was left to complete his reports and be reassigned to other duties. He retired before that happened. Seemingly, he had no desire for a second career.

By the time historians got around to writing about the western surveys, Wheeler's files had become so fragmented and incomplete as to leave historians dependent upon the annual and final reports. Those reports, though considered primary sources, have led to conclusions about Wheeler and his surveys that can be challenged.

This book begins with a brief introduction to Wheeler and his family from genealogical sources, then skips to the beginning years of his career in San Francisco, where he was sent following graduation in 1866 from the U.S. Military Academy at West Point. Assigned to the Army Corps of Engineers, Chief of Engineers Gen. A. A. Humphreys sent him to the corps's San Francisco office to assist in harbor and coastline surveys and defense construction. In 1868, at the request of Gen. E. O. C. Ord, who had recently been put in command of the army's California Department, Humphreys permitted Wheeler to join Ord's staff on a temporary basis.

In 1869, under Ord's direction, Wheeler conducted what he later publicized as his first survey west of the one hundredth meridian. It was not a survey, it was a reconnaissance. Furthermore, Wheeler did not use *survey* or *exploration* in the title of his report published early in 1870 or in the revision published in 1875. The words *west of the 100th meridian* were first used by Congress in 1872 when it passed the act of June 10, mandating the mapping of public lands west of the one hundredth meridian.

Wheeler returned to San Francisco late in 1869 from southeastern Nevada, where the focus for the entire five-month expedition had been primarily on mining districts, their access to transportation routes, and the disposition of the Nevada Indians. At that time he wrote the seldom-quoted twenty-page typewritten report published by Ord in 1870. Wheeler attached to this report three pages of tables with related data and a map of the region and sent this assemblage to Humphreys. Later that year Ord urged Humphreys to have the report published in folio form. When it finally appeared in 1875, it included extraneous material that had not been a part of the 1869 reconnaissance and excluded Wheeler's map of his itinerary and some of his personal remarks about Indians and Mormons. Those documents and others upon which this author relied were not with the Wheeler files but with miscellaneous correspondence at the National Archives that related to various aspects of War and Interior Department explorations and surveys.

Also at the National Archives is correspondence not in the Wheeler files that mentions an expedition Ord planned for Wheeler in 1870 that did not materialize. Furthermore, there is correspondence between Wheeler and others that gives the origin of the 1871 expedition and reveals that Wheeler was not ordered by Humphreys to undertake that expedition as had been believed.

Wheeler's career took a strange turn soon after he was assigned to General Ord. His assignments in 1869 and 1870 appear to have been arranged by Ord to please San Francisco's mining, mercantile, and banking interests. General Humphreys seems to have been in much the same position as General Ord: Neither was in a position to say no to San Francisco's leading capitalists because those special interests had direct access to some of the most influential men in Congress. This is supported by Wheeler's letter of January 23, 1871, to a congressman that

(facing page)

The pack-animal trail between Lee's Ferry and the lower crossing of the San Juan River at Navajo Ford, now crossed by a bridge to Mexican Hat, is shown here as the Buzzard's High Line.

Courtesy, National Park Service, U.S. Department of the Interior.

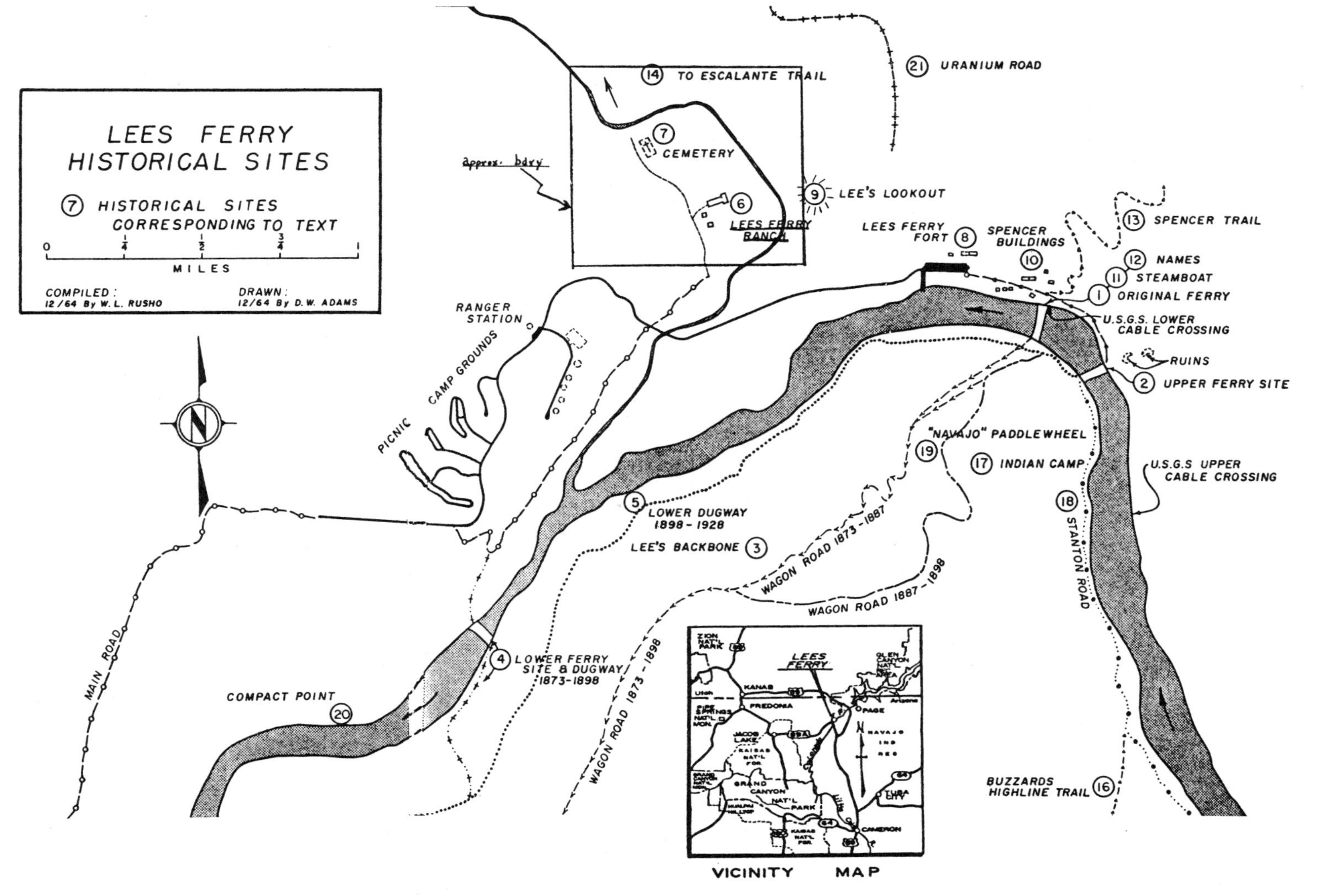
LEES FERRY
HISTORICAL SITES
7 HISTORICAL SITES
CORRESPONDING TO TEXT
0 1/4 1/2 3/4 1
MILES
COMPILED:
12/64 By W. L. RUSHO
DRAWN:
12/64 By D. W. ADAMS
14 TO ESCALANTE TRAIL
21 URANIUM ROAD
7 CEMETERY
approx. bdry
9 LEE'S LOOKOUT
6 LEES FERRY RANCH
LEES FERRY FORT 8
SPENCER BUILDINGS
10
13 SPENCER TRAIL
12 NAMES
11 STEAMBOAT
1 ORIGINAL FERRY
U.S.G.S. LOWER CABLE CROSSING
RUINS
2 UPPER FERRY SITE
RANGER STATION
CAMP GROUNDS
PICNIC
"NAVAJO" PADDLEWHEEL
19
17 INDIAN CAMP
U.S.G.S UPPER CABLE CROSSING
18
STANTON ROAD
5 LOWER DUGWAY
1898 - 1928
LEE'S BACKBONE 3
WAGON ROAD 1873 - 1887
WAGON ROAD 1887 - 1898
MAIN ROAD
4 LOWER FERRY SITE & DUGWAY
1873-1898
WAGON ROAD 1873 - 1898
COMPACT POINT
20
BUZZARDS HIGHLINE TRAIL 16
LEES FERRY
KANAB
FREDONIA
PAGE
JACOB LAKE
GRAND CANYON NAT'L PARK
CAMERON
VICINITY MAP

urged that he, Wheeler, be assigned to Washington, D.C., as soon as possible so that he could meet with congressional committees and obtain support for his 1871 expedition.

Not enough is known about Wheeler's formative years to write knowingly about what motivated him. The 1870 report supports what historians have suspected: Wheeler wished to be on a pedestal with John Wesley Powell, so his 1871 expedition included a boat trip to the Grand Canyon. Wheeler may also have wished for wealth which, for military men, was unattainable. His hidden agenda probably took form soon after he arrived in San Francisco, but so covertly did he operate that his mining operations did not come to light until the 1960s. His San Francisco mining company was formed without fanfare in Washington, D.C., with assistance from Sen. William Morris Stewart.

It has been the lot of historians to evaluate the contributions of Wheeler, Powell, Hayden, and King without knowing much about what went on behind the scenes during the months these survey leaders directed the fieldwork of their parties. Western newspapers supplied information of their whereabouts when known and occasionally elaborated on incidental happenings that were considered newsworthy. Mainly historians have relied on the published reports of the leaders, official correspondence, and secondary sources.

Wheeler is a particularly difficult subject because his reports attracted little favorable comment, much of his official correspondence and some of his record books are missing, and information in secondary sources is rather meager. This treatment of Wheeler fills in some of the gaps and calls attention to valuable sources of little-used information that separate the man from the myth.

ONE

The Brightest and the Best

GEORGE MONTAGUE WHEELER'S LIFE began in Massachusetts, where he was born in Hopkinton on October 9, 1842, to Miriam Daniels Wheeler and her husband John. John Wheeler was from a Grafton, Massachusetts, family whose lineage in America can be traced to 1676. It was to Grafton that the Wheelers moved after the births of their seven children, of which George was the fifth.[1]

In Grafton there were influential Wheelers to whom George was related, but his assist into the U.S. Military Academy at West Point is said to have come from a Colorado legislator. Graduating sixth in the class of 1866, Wheeler's aptitude for mathematics and engineering made him a likely prospect for the Army Corps of Engineers, which often obtained the brightest and best. The corps sent him to San Francisco to work as an assistant engineer, constructing defenses and surveying the harbor and coastline.

In April 1868 Gen. E. O. C. Ord arrived in San Francisco to take command of the Military Department of California. The proximity of his office to that of the corps led to an early meeting with Wheeler, and Wheeler became the beneficiary of Ord's customary assistance to young officers.[2]

Several months after meeting Wheeler, Ord applied to Chief of Engineers Gen. A. A. Humphreys for an engineer officer to survey military reservations in Arizona Territory. Ord designated a preference for Wheeler. In September Wheeler joined Ord's staff on a temporary basis.[3] After Wheeler completed the military reservation surveys in 1869, Ord obtained approval from Humphreys to send Wheeler and Lt. Daniel Lockwood, Wheeler's West Point classmate,[4] on a reconnaissance of eastern Nevada.[5] Lockwood served as Wheeler's assistant, except when Wheeler gave him executive command of a side party.

Late in November Wheeler and Lockwood, after five months of reconnoitering in Nevada, returned to San Francisco and wrote fascinating reports of their adventures. The high point for Wheeler was to stand on the bank of the Colorado River where John Wesley Powell had disembarked from his "perilous journey" in August.[6] On February 10, 1870, Wheeler forwarded their reports to General Humphreys.[7]

Historians relying mainly on the edited version of those reports, published in 1875 under the title, *Preliminary Report upon a Reconnaissance through Southern and Southeastern Nevada, Made in 1869,* have been deprived of certain of Wheeler's less-than-circumspect remarks that appear only in the original. Also omitted was Wheeler's earlier reference to Powell's "perilous journey."

When Wheeler, at the age of 23, arrived in San Francisco, the city was alive with mining excitement. Its capitalists, no longer enthusiastic about California's gold fields, had turned to Nevada's mountains of silver. Extraordinary wealth was coming from the Comstock to build impressive mansions and posh hotels. As the journalist Lucius Beebe said of San Francisco's "Golden Era," it wasn't love that made the world go round, it was money.[8] If the prospect of wealth went to Wheeler's head, he was not alone in planning how to acquire it. If he was a tool of the mining entrepreneurs, so was Ord. In fact, the 1869 reconnaissance survey seems to have been a cover for prospecting, initiated by Ord to oblige the mining industry.

Ord tended to be obliging. Furthermore, his lengthy periods of military service in California, begun in 1847, included not only the Gold Rush years but also the early years of silver mining in Nevada. Said to have had "many friends and acquaintances but perhaps no intimates,"[9] he would have known many prominent San Franciscans. Neither he nor other military leaders based in San Francisco could have escaped involvement in mining, if only to protect the mining interests from the Indians. The American public expected the federal government to assist in whatever form was essential to their economic well-being. Mining entrepreneurs were especially demanding. As powerful constituents of California congressmen, they had unimpeded access to the highest levels of government.

Special Orders No. 94, dated June 7, 1869, directed Wheeler to make a reconnaissance via Nevada's White Pine Mining District through the country south and east of there, and if practicable, to go "as far as the head of navigation on the Colorado River, with a view to opening a road thereto." Wheeler also was to obtain correct data for a military map, select sites for one or more military posts to protect the mines from hostile Indians, note the disposition of the Indians toward the settlers, and ascertain the resources available for future mining camps. The multipurpose wording of No. 94 differed little from that used to obtain congressional funding for explorations as far back as the 1820s and 1830s.[10]

What is of concern here is that funding for Wheeler's fact-finding trip largely duplicated the work of the Treasury Department's Rossiter Raymond, special commissioner of mining statistics. Raymond was then covering the same mining districts and providing in annual reports the same kinds of information about mine development, transportation routes, and the disposition of the various Indian tribes.[11] Only Wheeler's map covering his itinerary constituted new information, and it was not reproduced in the 1875 edition of Wheeler's 1869 reconnaissance.

Wheeler began his reconnaissance at Camp Ruby, Nevada, on July 13, 1869. His train consisted of thirty-six people, eight wagons, forty-eight mules, and thirty-one horses. About thirty of his men were escort soldiers, a rather large number in Indian country where, according to Raymond, the Indians were friendly. In addition to Lieutenant Lockwood, Wheeler's professional staff consisted of assistant surgeon John D. Hall, U.S. Army; topographer Peter Hamel; William Ord, the general's brother; and Carl Rahsskopff of the San Francisco instrument firm of Rahsskopff & Riedinger. In the report, Wheeler mentioned that Ord did some sketching and Rahsskopff did some photography. Apparently Rahsskopff came along because he could assist Hamel, having knowledge of mapping instruments and topographic mensuration. Dr. Hall examined "flora of the country passed through."[12]

Wheeler and Lockwood visited eighteen mining districts, and it is likely that they were wined and dined at the thriving ones. At others, there was little or nothing going on. In the remote southeastern part of the state, they separated. Wheeler wanted to satisfy his curiosity about the early Mormon settlements in the mountain valleys, isolated by roads so rough that few traveled them, while Lockwood took part of Wheeler's party to Hiko and then to Pahranagat Valley. They were to rendezvous at the Virgin River.

With ambulance and heavy wagon Lockwood traveled twenty-one miles on the first day before making camp. On the second day he came to wagon tracks going off "in every direction" and followed the wrong ones. Two days later he was back at the first night's camp, his wagon twenty-five miles out in the desert. The rest of his party arrived the following morning with the wagon and the team of mules, the latter in a broken-down condition. Other problems he encountered before reaching Hiko were bad water and more bad roads. To make up for lost time he visited only one mining camp near Hiko, estimated the combined population as between 250 and 300 "souls," and headed for Pahranagat Lake. En route he noted "quite a number of ranches in good condition."[13]

During that period Wheeler also lost time, slowed by almost impassable roads. Eventually he reached Homer in upper Ursine Valley, where he was met by the "Bishop, or acting businessman of the colony." Homer was "built in the shape of a fort," Wheeler said, and added that it was "settled with a number of those provincial ignorant people of the Mormon persuasion." (More such derogatory remarks about Indians as well as Mormons appear in the 1869 report than in the 1875 edition.) Of historic importance is Wheeler's account of settlements that would soon be vacated by order of Brigham Young, who was then recalling these far-flung followers to Utah. Very few of those early settlements survived.[14]

En route to Pioche, Nevada, Wheeler passed through Eagle Valley, where he saw "fine agricultural crops," and Rose Valley, where he saw Mormon ranchers and many head of stock. Then he visited Pioche, named for Francis Pioche, the San Francisco importer and mining entrepreneur who later figured in Wheeler's mining scheme. Located in the thriving Ely Mining District, it was a town in which Wheeler could expect to be royally entertained.[15]

Leaving Pioche, Wheeler passed a Mormon settlement with "some seven or eight hundred acres of arable land" and a small sawmill which the Mormons had built to supply their settlements with lumber. Continuing on his way he began looking for signs of Lockwood and party, fearing they were out of rations. Walking with William Ord, whose mount had given out, and still far distant from the planned rendezvous on the Virgin River, Wheeler climbed a sand dune for a better look. In the distance he saw what appeared to be an encampment. It was Lockwood's, and as he had feared, the party was out of provisions. With Lockwood, Wheeler traveled eighteen more miles to the nearest Mormon village on the Muddy River to procure food and grain.[16]

Wheeler called the valley of the Muddy River the "Dixie of Nevada," noting that the richness of its soil served a population of from twelve to fifteen hundred people. As noted above, within the next few years the Mormons would abandon their villages of West Point, St. Joseph, and St. Thomas, which thereafter became ghost towns. (In this century two of them were inundated by Lake Mead.) Of the residents, Wheeler wrote that during summer months many of the men went "to the more northern settlements, to return again in the winter, having always, as a matter of course, a wife or wives in each place." One of the men he described as "privileged with four wives, . . . the happy father of twenty-two children" and all of them at this "winter resort being reared unwashed, unkempt, untaught."[17]

Wheeler devoted most of his report to mining districts and mining opportunities. With seeming authority he discussed the prospects of each district, but as it turned out later, his enthusiasm or lack thereof was often misplaced. He was better at describing scenery. Note his eloquent description of the Colorado River canyons he visited after leaving the Mormon villages on the Muddy: "The mountain scenery in this locality, to my idea was the most wild, picturesque and pleasing of any that it has ever been my fortune to meet. The walls of the Black Cañon rise steep, dark and sharp on the south and east, and to the northeast those of Boulder Cañon . . . are perpendicular, from twelve to fifteen hundred feet in height. The scene encountered upon reaching the river by moonlight, after threading a steep and sandy wash, was one of extreme loneliness and grandeur."[18]

TWO

Origins

THE 1870 NEVADA-ARIZONA SURVEY that General Ord planned for Wheeler is virtually unknown. It was scheduled to begin in October and continue for six months. Maj. Gen. J. M. Schofield agreed to supply $10,000 from his account to defray the cost of employing civilian assistants. Gen. A. A. Humphreys, chief of the Army Corps of Engineers, approved the hiring of two topographers and two assistant topographers. In a letter to Humphreys dated September 9, Wheeler asked permission to hire the photographer Timothy H. O'Sullivan to serve as a topographer. O'Sullivan had been Clarence King's photographer on the fortieth parallel survey which Humphreys had approved in 1867. The well-qualified Swiss topographer Henry Custer, hired by Wheeler, also had been with the King survey. The record does not disclose whether Wheeler hired two assistant topographers; their names do not appear in the correspondence.[1]

About the time Wheeler was ready to leave San Francisco to conduct the survey, Schofield sought a postponement because the $10,000 was needed for a more pressing purpose. The secretary of war approved the postponement on November 5, but not until December was Wheeler told "to discharge all employe's engaged for this exploration." Custer and O'Sullivan, each hired at $150 per month, filed claims for loss of wages. From Custer's claim we learn the sequence of events.

When Custer's lawyer brought the matter before the secretary of war, Humphreys was asked to comment. After quoting Ord as saying that Custer and O'Sullivan "were not entitled to pay beyond what had already been received by them," Humphreys explained that it was "the custom to hire by the month, the engagement terminating at any day at the option of either party for cause and no greater cause can exist than the subsequent abandonment of an expedition by orders of a superior."[2]

Humphreys, a respected scientist as well as a capable administrator, was one of the original fifty members of the National Academy of Sciences, incorporated in 1863 by Congress as an advisory body to whom it could turn for scientific expertise and advice. He had earned his laurels when he was a captain in the Corps of Topographical Engineers, assigned in 1851 to study the Mississippi River delta. The "long hours he devoted to field work" brought on exhaustion and caused a delay in the project. With assistance from Lt. H. L. Abbot, appointed in 1857, the work was completed in 1860 and published the following year. Their 610-page report became an immediate best-seller, with parts of it "translated into many languages." Humphreys is remembered today for his contributions to the field of hydrology.[3]

In 1853 Congress passed funding legislation "to ascertain the most practicable and economical route for a railway from the Mississippi River to the Pacific Ocean." Humphreys became the administrator of the explorations and surveys by the officers of the Topographic Corps that became known as the Pacific Railroad Reports, a twelve-volume series that began appearing in 1855.[4]

In 1867 Humphreys—more scientist than bureaucrat—quickly approved King's plan to survey a strip one hundred miles wide along the fortieth parallel between Nevada and Colorado that included the Central Pacific rail line, then in progress. Furthermore, he gave King a free hand to hire his own staff and write his own orders. He did no less in 1871 when Wheeler sought approval for surveys to be conducted south of King's fortieth-parallel survey.

The aborted 1870 survey can be said to be the genesis of Wheeler's 1871 survey. Not only had it brought Wheeler's considerable backing by Ord and Schofield to Humphreys's attention but it also brought congressional support, including some from an unexpected quarter. While awaiting reassignment to Washington, Wheeler wrote Congressman Logan Roots of Arkansas asking Roots to intercede on his behalf with Humphreys, who appeared to be in no hurry to get the 1871 survey under way.[5] (See Appendix C.)

Wheeler told Roots that an official recommendation had gone to Washington that he be "ordered" there to meet "personally the members of the various committees under whose especial eye come the interests of the Pacific Coast in the way of development of mines & such other resources. . . ." Wheeler emphasized that the "Pacific Delegation" was very much in favor of a continuance of his work.

Of course it was. Nevada's senator William Morris Stewart, who later, in 1872, facilitated the formation of Lyons and Wheeler Mining Company, and other western congressmen were in Washington to serve the mining interests. Stewart's credentials for election to the Senate included experience in California, where he had specialized in mining litigation. An avid though largely unsuccessful speculator in mining prospects such as Wheeler's, he made his money in court.[6]

Wheeler's request to Roots that he advise members of the Pacific Delegation that Wheeler was eager to leave for Washington, D.C., had the desired effect. On February 2, Roots sent Wheeler's letter to Humphreys with a note saying, "I feel very much interested in his success & that of his expedition, and should be glad to give all the aid in my power. I hope you will favorably consider his request and suggestions."[7]

Wheeler was ambiguous about the origin of his surveys. Usually he said he had been ordered to undertake them. But the plan he submitted to Humphreys for the 1871 season's fieldwork dated February 21 was not materially revised, except for Humphreys's omission of "eastern California" in his instructions of March 23. Special Orders No. 109, attached to Humphreys's instructions, confined Wheeler to "those portions of the United States territory lying south of the Central Pacific Railroad embracing parts of eastern Nevada and Arizona." Whatever the intent of these orders, Wheeler was not the first officer to exceed his.[8]

Wheeler had $50,000 at his disposal for the 1871–72 fiscal year. Most of that would go to pay and maintain in the field his civilian assistants. Special Orders No. 109 provided for their transportation and an escort; assumed responsibility for procuring animals and forage; supplied subsistence stores, instruments, etc.; and included "the necessary rations and antiscorbutics for the party." It provided a medical officer, two hospital stewards, and the necessary medical stores and supplied "horse equipments, arms and ammunition at such points as may be necessary."[9]

By May Wheeler had engaged most of his staff, including two chief topographers: one at $194 per month, at the top of the salary scale for civilian assistants; chief geologist G. K. Gilbert and photographer Timothy O'Sullivan, each at $150; and artist Edward Richardson, employed as assistant surveyor, at $83.33.[10] Artists not specifically assigned to other duties were not carried on the government's payroll. Usually they joined the western surveys for fresh subject matter offered by firsthand exposure to an unsettled, sometimes dangerous, but extraordinarily beautiful region beyond the one hundredth meridian. Richardson had seen a great deal of British Columbia, where he had painted for several years before moving to San Francisco in 1868. In California he had made numerous sketching trips.[11] Wheeler's preference for color in depicting western scenery as much as his desire to compete on equal terms with other survey leaders prompted him to seek a landscape painter, even one without impressive credentials. Richardson, the son of a London sculptor, was still a struggling artist when Wheeler met him, possibly at one of San Francisco's occasional art exhibitions.

Although the record establishes that Richardson made some sketches while in Wheeler's employ, it is not known what became of them or even what became of Richardson after Wheeler issued disbanding orders in November at Fort Whipple, Arizona. Probably most, if not all, of the sketches were lost to the Colorado River in October when Wheeler's boat capsized. If so, Wheeler may not have wanted to admit this to Humphreys, to whom he said that such sketching as had been done was that of "amateurs" and that "the only results that [could] serve as valuable adjuncts to a report" were the photographs of the Colorado River canyons.[12] Fortunately O'Sullivan had possession of those.

Because Wheeler had to reconstruct his field notes mostly from memory, they represent a retrospective view that may be more fictional than factual. Therefore, his book of special field orders and circulars and Gilbert's field notes are more useful in learning about the 1871 expedition. Gilbert was in charge of "geological studies and collections, and the general direction of any Assistant Geologist . . . or of any talent of this nature that may be developed." His suggestions were to be received by persons working in "the different branches of Natural History" with a view to furthering a "full geological examination." This is rather a large order for a young geologist who had no prior experience in the study of western geology. Intent on doing a thorough investigation, he was not prepared to fall in line with Wheeler's plan to cover ninety-two mining districts and obtain answers to forty-five questions that had little to do with scientific analyses of geologic formations.[13]

Wheeler wanted to know the dates the mining districts were discovered; whether the mines had been worked at intervals or continuously; the names of the recorders for each county; the names of the postmasters and Wells Fargo agents; the distances of the mines from the railroad; geographic descriptions of boundary lines for each district; the positions of mining ledges in relation to the main mountain ranges; average costs per ton for mining, milling, and roasting the ore; the prices of grain and hay, and so on. Was this data for mining entrepreneurs, or did Wheeler think that it would enable him to write a statistical report to the credit of the War Department that would match that of Rossiter Raymond's for the Treasury Department? Or did he wish to match or surpass the value of Clarence King's report, *Mining Industry,*[14] which had come out in 1870? (The latter, called in 1871 the "most valuable contribution yet made to the literature on the Mining Industry in the United States,"[15] was a product of King's survey of the fortieth parallel, begun in 1867 and financed by the War Department.)

Gilbert's notebooks begin with the third week of April when he was en route to San Francisco. At Halleck Station, Nevada, on the Central Pacific line, he stopped off to talk with one of Wheeler's men and to pick up a list of personnel engaged for the expedition. Reaching San Francisco on the twenty-ninth, he went directly to the Mercantile Library to read up on earlier expeditions in the West, making a complete list of them. It was typical of Gilbert to be thorough.

Back in Nevada a few days later, Gilbert spent some time at Camp Halleck. His notebook entry for May 12 indicates misgivings about military discipline. A note he wrote to Wheeler, possibly in protest, is crossed out. A mule had drowned for which the soldier in charge was to be punished.[16] Had Gilbert protested the nature of the punishment to Wheeler? Was this incident the beginning of the antipathy they felt for each other? Far more serious incidents of which Gilbert must have been aware were to follow, but none of them appear in the almost daily entries in his notebooks. To learn of them one must turn to the *Inyo Independent* of Independence, California. Dated November 18, 1871, and entitled "Wheeler and His Guides—Where Is Egan"? the article dealt with missing guides, abused Indians, and powers of attorney that Wheeler had induced his men to sign. "Did the Government fit out a private prospecting expedition?" inquired the *Independent.*[17]

Wheeler opened the 1871 field season short of executive officers. Lt. D. A. Lyle did not report for duty until late June; Lt. D. W. Lockwood, not until late July. On May 15 Wheeler issued Special Field Orders No. 3, the only order of record issued by Wheeler in 1871 that gave civilian assistants executive command of a party; it assigned G. K. Gilbert and Timothy O'Sullivan "co-equal powers of authority in the execution of the work called for."[18] With several other civilian assistants and an escort of seven privates and a corporal, they made field investigations until they rejoined Wheeler at Belmont on June 8. Their associations with central Nevada's Indians during that period were not eventful, except for the appearance in camp one night of "Gen Breckenridge, Chief of the Paiutes," who presented "his credentials."[19]

At Belmont, Wheeler gave Gilbert instructions to examine another mining area, this time without O'Sullivan, who probably remained with Wheeler at Belmont. (Belmont's population in 1868 had reached two thousand, but it had dwindled in size after the discovery of silver at White Pine. It regained its importance as a mining and trading center, functioning as such until well into the twentieth century. Later it was to become one of Nevada's most interesting ghost towns.)[20] From Belmont, Gilbert went to Toiyabe City, at that time already a ghost town. Located in Ophir Canyon, where silver was discovered by a Frenchman in 1863, Toiyabe City had a population of several hundred that was served by triweekly stage runs to and from Austin, Nevada. After the principal mine went bankrupt in 1869 nearly everyone moved away. Gilbert found a town of fifty houses and only four or five inhabitants. All were French, except one.[21]

Apparently in Gilbert's absence, Wheeler laid down the law by putting into effect Articles 60 and 96 of the *Rules and Articles of War*. Issuance of Circular No. 1 in Wheeler's book of special orders may have been prompted by the reaction of some of his men to his mistreatment of a young Indian boy, who allegedly was "tied by the thumbs to an elevated wagon tongue."[22] The story given the *Independent* was that one of Wheeler's mules had strayed or was stolen, that soldiers sent in search of the mule were told to bring back the first Indians they found, and that they found this Indian boy herding cattle. The basic decency of most of Wheeler's men would have caused them to be outraged by such an act. Had any of them intervened, Wheeler would not have taken it lightly.

Among Wheeler's officers and men were surgeons, hospital stewards, mineralogists, astronomical observers, naturalists, topographers, geologists, and others. One can only imagine their reactions to a warning that Articles 60 and 96 of the *Rules and Articles of War* would be "strictly enforced," and that they applied "to all civilian assistants, and employe's connected with this Expedition." Article 60 states that "all sutlers and retainers of the camp, and all persons whatsoever, serving with the armies of the United States in the field, though not enlisted soldiers, are to be subject to orders according to the rules and discipline of war." Article 96 states that "all officers, conductors, gunners, matrosses, drivers, or other persons whatsoever, receiving pay or hire in the service of the Artillery or Corps of Engineers of the United States, shall be governed by the aforesaid Rules and Articles and shall be subject to be tried by courts-martial, in like manner with the Officers and soldiers of the other troops in the service of the United States."[23]

It is of course possible that Wheeler never delivered his ultimatum, but neither is it crossed out in the circular. It is, however, evident in Gilbert's notes that he did not again take a position when he witnessed circumstances that ordinarily would evoke comment. Unfortunately, his notes constitute the only daily reporting known to exist.

Combining Gilbert's notes, newspaper accounts, and Wheeler's 1871–73 book of special orders, special field orders, and circulars with his annual reports is essential to obtain a reasonably accurate appraisal of what was going on during those years. To what extent Wheeler let his desire for information on mineral deposits dictate the pace of his survey, or "reconnaissance" as Gilbert called it, is open to conjecture. Wheeler has been criticized and condemned, defended and praised for the number of square miles he said he surveyed: 78,950 in 1871. To cover that much territory, he distributed his men widely and kept them at a fast pace. Gilbert considered the pace too fast. It seems likely that data collected under such conditions might well account for the poor quality of Wheeler's maps. Covering so much territory also necessitated sending men out alone, placing them at risk from natural hazards or desperate men.

Gilbert recalled working alone, ill with a cold, in the wildly beautiful and rugged Pahranagat region of Nevada, known then to be a haven for horse thieves and other desperadoes.[24] After two days, fortunately without incident, he went on to Hiko, where he reported that the Mormons had "left or backslid," and the stagnation of mining had rendered the town "fearfully dull." There, on July 13, he was joined by Wheeler for a trip to Pioche. At Pahroc Spring, where some mines had been located, they stopped for a visit with O'Sullivan.[25]

Gilbert then joined a small party headed for Wheeler's supply depot at Camp Independence, California. En route they passed through the northern part of Death Valley in the general area where Lieutenant Lyle's guide, Charles C. F. R. Hahn, failed to return to camp after having been sent in search of water. Hahn was familiar with the mining trails and water holes in this area and was not likely to have become lost. His friends reported to the *Independent* that they had found his "saddle, blanket, shirts, saddle blankets, the buckle of his army belt, with letters and papers" at Gold Mountain near the head of Death Valley. They thought he had been "disabled while out of camp and left to perish." An "attache" of Lyle's party "on his return [to Independence] told a well-known citizen of the Valley, that we would never see Hahn again, for [John] Koehler said he would go out with him to 'make him find the water or kill him.' "[26]

When Lyle returned to Camp Independence from northern Death Valley, Wheeler engaged for him as guide, William Egan, a well-known local resident who had some mines in the newly created Granite Mountain District near Darwin Canyon at the west entrance of Death Valley. Wheeler sent Lyle to report on mines in that area and to conduct topographic work in the vicinity of Telescope Peak where Wheeler would join him. Lyle camped at Rose Spring, about five miles from the peak. His mules were in bad shape and apparently so was his water supply. With his party but not on Wheeler's payroll was Charles King, a Nevada resident, whom Lyle sent to find a feasible route by which the party could proceed to Furnace Creek on the other side of the valley. He sent Egan, O'Sullivan, and a packer named Price to intercept Wheeler and bring him to Rose Spring. On or about August 20, O'Sullivan and Price returned to Lyle's camp without Egan. Wheeler who had been looking for mining prospects, apparently with John Koehler, reached Lyle's camp a day or so later but did not send out a search party, nor had he done so when Hahn disappeared. In his report he presumed both guides had lost their way.[27]

Death Valley at the time of Wheeler's report included a larger area than does the national monument that was established there in 1933. Lockwood and his parties explored and did topographical work in the southern part during most of August. Gilbert was under Lockwood's command. On August 18 he described what it was like in the valley when water holes were reduced to mud and springs to trickles.

> Our dry camp of last night illustrated some phases of human nature good & bad. There was no conversion of character, but merely a development. Those who customarily exhibited sense remained cool. The feeble minded were panic stricken. The generous, the selfish, the sanguine, the timid did not change their characters. The animals were all tied up and offered barley of which about half of them partook. Water was of course hoarded most carefully. No washing of hands or dishes was allowed. The little remaining of the kegful after making tea for supper & bkfst. was poured into the most reduced canteens. The greed with which one or two absorbed the public water showed that it would not do to make it common property in case of extremity. The only way to ensure a proper economy & temperance in its use is

> to have each canteenful private property, &, if a larger quantity is transported, to have it issued in rations in some equitable manner.
>
> The water in these holes but half satisfies the thirst of our brutes. Individual care gives a good drink to each riding animal, but the pack train is still too thirsty to eat. The quietness with which they stand all night in line at the Apparahoes [aparejos] is a striking illustration of the power of discipline.[28]

Gilbert, too, was disciplined. His notes do not dwell on Death Valley's oppressive heat, which ranged from 120 to 128 degrees in the shade, nor the long night marches in search of water. But on the way out, August 25, he noted his impression: "Death Valley has a characteristic look to the North—steep sided, hazy, deep, repellant."[29]

Gilbert was in camp at Cottonwood Springs, Nevada, when topographer Louis Nell failed to return from the vicinity of Saratoga Springs, where he had been working alone. Two days later he was found "senseless & lying on his face with his mouth half full of sand." William Lyons, one of Wheeler's blacksmiths, reported that it had taken him a half hour to get Nell to swallow and another half hour before Nell could speak. Having refreshed him "a little with water and whiskey, Lyons went on to Saratoga Springs & met Marvine & returned with food & [Private I.] Hutchins. They took Nell to Salt Spr. & he was there taken into the wagon."[30] (A. R. Marvine was a prominent geologist serving as astronomical assistant.)

When Gilbert entered the details in his notebook on August 31, he was clearly upset, especially by the behavior of A. H. Cochrane. "Dr. Cochrane has the atrocious taste to continually abuse Nell (absent) for stupidity in getting sick & getting lost." But Gilbert did not report what else was happening at Cottonwood Springs on August 31. Special Field Orders No. 21 called for a "council of administration [to] convene at this camp, today, at 11 a.m., or as soon thereafter as practicable to dispose of the effects of the late Egan, citizen guide, attached to Lieut Wheeler's Expdn."[31]

Fred Loring, a Boston short story writer serving as Wheeler's secretary, was one of the last persons to see Egan alive. Whether it was loyalty to Wheeler that prompted Loring to handle the matter as he did or a desire to amuse readers of *Appleton's Journal of Literature* is not known. When James Brady, an Inyo County mining engineer, tried to find out what had happened to his friend Egan, Loring was vague and uncommunicative.[32] In November 1871, however, he purported to know all about it and in addition supplied a description of Egan that did not fit

Egan's character. Even if it had, it was grossly inappropriate under the circumstances. The article quotes verbatim from Loring's diary. An entry for August 18 reads: "Our guide left today with S______ to try some of the cañons on the west side of the Death Valley for water so that we can cross over easily to Furnace Creek; and for a short time we have a respite from bear-stories," a reference to an earlier entry. There is general agreement that the "S" refers to O'Sullivan, often written as "Sullivan." Apropos the bear stories, Loring said, "We have a guide, an objectionable pioneer, mountaineer, miner, forty-niner, bear-hunter, and squatter. I do not like the class. . . . He is ubiquitous in camp, and has kept me actively away from reach of his saliva—the beast! He will tell bear-stories, and roar in immitation of a grizzly while doing it, which is not pleasant."

According to Loring's diary, O'Sullivan returned to camp on August 20. On August 21, Loring said, "S______ arrived in camp last night, with no guide. He was a fraud—such a fraud as only an old mountaineer who pretends to know the country can be. After leading them fairly into Death Valley, he left them, as they found he had lost his way. He did not come back again, and he never will come back."[33]

The *Independent* took Loring to task: "In his zealous severity Mr. Loring made this guide father expressions which might have emanated from Hahn, but never from Egan. While Hahn's brusque disposition may have inspired Wheeler's sophomores with dislike, [Egan's] profound classical education and infinitely superior linguistic attainments would quite possibly incite feelings of envy." Several weeks later the *Independent* received a letter from Lyle that also belied Loring's description of Egan.[34]

In November, Peter Monto, a resident of Inyo County who had been Lyle's blacksmith, suggested to the *Independent* that Wheeler had made some mining locations in the area of Egan's disappearance and hinted "of a possible collision between the two."[35] Monto said that Koehler had been with Wheeler. Koehler (also spelled Kohler) had been hired as a collector in natural history. It is doubtful that he possessed any knowledge of natural history aside from the ability to spot good mining prospects. A desiccated body thought to be Egan's was later seen along a trail in that vicinity by V. A. Gregg, who was searching for a lead deposit that had been remarked on by Wheeler.[36]

Typical of reports that need to put a good face on things, Wheeler glossed over the missing guides. Nor did he mention the Indians, except to say that they were "surly." However he did not escape censure for an incident that happened at Ash Meadows, either in Inyo County or in Washington. The first exposure came from the *Independent*, which relied on Peter Monto's information. Monto reported that Wheeler was in camp at Ash Meadows, Nevada, when he asked an Indian to take a note to Wheeler's brother, Willard, whom he had put in charge of supplies at Camp Independence. Wheeler needed a fresh supply of mules. The Indian asked for a "shirt, pair of pants and $5." Wheeler refused, and the Indian left without the note but returned the following morning with four of his friends to negotiate further. Wheeler ordered them tied to the ground. They attempted to escape after one of them broke free. They were then fired upon, killing one and blinding another.[37]

The incident came to light again in 1874 when John Wesley Powell was deprecating the use of escort soldiers on survey trips during his testimony before the Committee on Public Lands in Washington, D.C. The presence of troups interfered with his study of Indian languages. He revealed that, while in Utah in 1872, he had learned why smoke signals had been sent following the incident at Ash Meadows. Powell told the committee that as soon as Wheeler "took the field, delegations of Indians came [to him] from Panamint Mountain near the California line, from Nevada, and from Utah, asking [him] whether the government had sent out an expedition to kill the Indians."[38]

Wheeler's conduct of this 1871 expedition suggests there was more to his plans than merely mapping a portion of the Southwest. The location of Camp Independence, Wheeler's supply depot, did not require Wheeler to cross the rugged Panamints. Neither Humphreys's letter to him of March 23, 1871, nor Special Orders No. 109, which Humphreys enclosed, prepares one to accept that Wheeler was adhering to orders when he sent Lyle to Telegraph Peak and Lockwood to Death Valley. Nor was there justification for his parties to be working in the hottest place in the nation during the hottest time of the year. The consequences of having done so took a heavy toll on mules and men. Wheeler's desperate need for a fresh supply of mules precipitated the incident at Ash Meadows. The formation of Lyons and Wheeler Mining Company early in 1872 suggests that the aim of acquiring mining locations in southeastern California may have been on Wheeler's hidden agenda.

Boomtowns had been waxing and waning in the vicinity of Camp Independence since its founding in 1862, among them Bend City. Located near the Owens River, Bend City soon acquired two hotels and sixty or more buildings. San Carlos and Chrysopolis grew up nearby. By 1865 the boom was over. The next town to appear was Independence, founded in 1866. When Wheeler arrived there in 1871, mining prospectors were looking to the Panamints for the next bonanza. The boom materialized several years later.

Towns located in the Panamints were Darwin and Panamint City. Darwin was named for Dr. Darwin French, who found silver and gold (some sources say silver and lead) in the Cosa Range twelve miles south while searching for the "lost gunsight lode" in 1859 with a party of prospectors. Eventually the town attained a population of fifteen hundred before it declined to less than one hundred.[39]

Panamint City, south of 11,045-foot Telescope Peak, reached a rumored population of twenty-five hundred before it was reduced to a ghost town after the price of silver declined in the 1930s.[40]

Most of the mining activity in the region was carried on in altitudes between four thousand and nine thousand feet above sea level. The altitude of the Panamints varies from about six thousand feet and higher, with Telescope Peak towering over the entire region. Across Death Valley are the Black Mountains, the Funeral Range, and at the northern end, the Grapevine Mountains, where Hahn disappeared. Far less rugged than the Panamints, their altitudes range from about four thousand to eight thousand feet. About five hundred square miles of the valley floor, or trough, are below sea level. The lowest place is at Badwater, almost two hundred eighty feet below sea level. In that valley and in the mountains that border it, Wheeler and his parties spent much of July and all of August.[41]

THREE

Bucking the Colorado

When Wheeler left Cottonwood Springs for the Colorado River about August 31, 1871, he placed Lieutenant Lockwood in charge of the "land parties" and turned his book of special orders over to Lieutenant Lyle. Lockwood was to proceed to Las Vegas Ranch en route to St. George, Utah; Lyle was to follow twenty-four hours later.[1] With them went Wheeler's prospectors, except for William McGeary, who went with Wheeler.

Wheeler and Gilbert were at Fort Mojave on September 12, and there Gilbert got his introduction to the "athletic & handsome, graceful" Indians for whom their reservation was named. He noted their crops of corn, melons, squash, and beans, which extended along the Colorado River where the flood waters could reach the land each year during the period of heavy runoff. On the sixteenth, with three boats and a barge, Wheeler began the ascent of the river. In Boat No. 1 were Wheeler, Fred Loring, William McGeary, one soldier, and three Mohave. In Boat No. 2 were Dr. W. J. Hoffman, Timothy O'Sullivan, George Phifer, William George Salmon, one soldier, and three Mohave. Gilbert's companions in Boat No. 3 were topographer Peter Hamel, artist and assistant surveyor Edward Richardson, hospital steward Frank Hecox, two soldiers, and three Mohave. On the barge which was to accompany the boats partway were five Mohave (including Asquit, their captain), two soldiers, and a boatman. "We started our boats from Mojave today at 11:35 am after having posed for a stereograph," said Gilbert.[2]

On September 21, O'Sullivan photographed Black Canyon. Having seen a sketch of it in the Joseph C. Ives report,[3] Gilbert found it "a little disappointing." He had expected higher and more perpendicular walls. Except for the winds that interfered with photographing them, O'Sullivan was in his element. Gilbert wrote down locations of the "Gilbralter" photographs taken at the gate of the canyon. Regarding the wind, he said that it "was of great service . . . , carrying us along gaily except at three or four rapids. *Contra,* it interfered with photography & kept O'Sullivan in a perpetual state of profanity."[4]

Still in Black Canyon on the twenty-third, O'Sullivan spent most of the day taking photographs. Gilbert said that the "cañon in this part better accords with the idea" he had conceived. "The walls are not so steep and fancy as . . . pictured [in the Ives report] nor are they so huge but they are for considerable distances unclimbable and we found camping ground so scarce that our search for it was prolonged into the darkness."[5]

On the twenty-fifth Gilbert wrote down the names of Indians who had posed with part of the boat crew: Eel-i-taw, Tah-wah-gah, and Itz-i-quah-rah, simplifying the spellings to Eelita, Tawaga-Owahna, and Itsiquara.

On October 1, O'Sullivan delayed the party until he could get a favorable light to photograph "the Cathedral." The boats and the barge got underway at 1 P.M. Late in the afternoon they came to a difficult rapid. Gilbert wrote that "navigation occupied so much attention" that he had little time for "the rock." Later he expressed his reservations about the way Wheeler's boat had been handled, comparing it unfavorably with the barge which was manned by the Mohave: "The superiority of management of the Barge, as compared with No. 1, was conspicuous as they went up this rapid where everyone put his best foot foremost."[6]

As prearranged, Wheeler met with the land parties on October 5. Some redistribution of men transpired before the barge was sent back to Fort Mojave and the land parties left to explore northeastern Arizona. Wheeler put O'Sullivan and Gilbert in charge of boats No. 2 and No. 3, respectively. O'Sullivan had been calling the boat with camera and photographic supplies *The Picture,* Gilbert named his boat *The Trilobite* and listed his crew as Edward M. Richardson, artist; Frank Hecox, meteorologist; Rich. W. James, cockswain; Thos. Hoagland, cook; Private Anthony [Arthur] Keegan; and 3 Mojave.[7] Hoagland was subsequently transferred to Boat No. 1 to be with Wheeler, perhaps to give Wheeler more control over the food supply.

At Camp No. 20 on October 8 Gilbert wrote down Wheeler's orders for an estimated sixty miles of river travel before the boat party could expect to reach Diamond River [Diamond Creek], where the voyage was to terminate on October 16. On the ninth, Gilbert counted fifteen rapids. Wheeler's boat had faltered at the last one, causing injury to William Roberts. On the tenth the rapids were fewer but higher, and the Mohave, Panambona, was badly bruised on the chest when he was thrown upon rocks. Miraculously, no one was injured on the eleventh when Wheeler's boat was destroyed and nearly all the contents washed away, including Wheeler's papers. In the final report Wheeler's description of what happened on the eleventh was phrased to obscure details. Gilbert, however, had no compunction about revealing what transpired:[8]

> We find as we proceed two long stretches of rowing water where the granite walls hold the river narrow with very little debris at the foot[;] a sharp rapid intervenes and at the head of the upper, a rousing rapid that gave us one too many.
>
> The leading boat [No. 1], McGeary at the helm; Hoagland at the pole—wrecked or rather swamped & upset scattering its freight along the bottom & top of the river. I started at once with Hecox, Salmon, Keegan & Drew as oarsmen to save the floating debris. We managed to pick up the oars & some blankets & baggage & others were saved along the shore but 3 or 4 beds, 3 p[ai]rs saddlebags & a considerable amt—nearly all the rations were lost. The most serious losses were those of the record of astronomical observations of Party 1 & of Lt. Wheeler's basket of papers & notebooks. My only loss is of the Macomb Expedition Map that Dr. Newberry gave me. Some of the men are demoralized a little by the rapid & tomorrow I have volunteered to steer a boat up.[9]
>
> Oct 12 Thurs. This book opens under a cloud at Camp 22 in the Big Cañon, for last night occurred the accident that lost valuable books & papers and this morning all hands are at work repairing & searching. As the Sextant books are lost I have given observations a place here. . . . In the P.M. after astronomical observations & caulking we take all the things up again to the rapids & with Mr. Wheeler for bowsman I take Boat Picture up the rapid. We ship water where McGeary did but the large force on the rope pulled us through safely. Our camp [is] at the head of the rapids.[10]
>
> Friday Oct 13. From this point & time the boat party is divided. . . . The Picture & Trilobite go on up with 10 men (7 white & black; 3 red) each. Salmon being sick & James demoralized I take the tiller in strong rapids & Hecox [is] my efficient as-

> sistant. During the day we make some lively transits. One involved a run out with the line on the tholepin & then a jerk ahead after throwing it off. The boat was often so highly inclined on a fall that to go forward one must climb as though upstairs.[11]

Saturday morning, October 14, Gilbert visited a creek opposite Camp No. 24, where he saw some Indian gardens. They were to be his only respite from another day of dangerous rapids. At noon the boat parties encountered the "worst rapid" they had met and were "compelled to make a portage of boats as well as freight." The river's current being too swift to row and the cliffs so perpendicular that towing was "out of the question," they "crept in the old Genesee style & laid a rope to warp up by with loaded boats."[12]

On Sunday, October 15, Gilbert took inventory of the provisions on his boat. (Daily rations for Indians were smaller and had less variety.)

	White	Red	Total
Flour lbs	20–5	25	45–50
Bacon lbs	0	1½	1½
Hard Bread lbs	1½	6½	8
Coffee lbs	2¼	2	4½
Sugar lbs	3	½	3½
Rice lbs	2½		2½
Pears cans	1		1
Beans lbs	0	1½	1½
Undivided coffee	8		8

After noting that *The Picture* was much better provisioned—Wheeler was with O'Sullivan—Gilbert said it was "doubtful" whether both boats could be fully rationed for more than five days. "The ration matter may yet turn us back." The day's work was a series of rapids, and progress was but four miles.[13]

Monday, October 16, during which the party covered only one and a half miles, was the day they were to have met the land parties at "Diamond River," later known as Diamond Creek. "Tonight," said Gilbert, "Lt Wheeler puts us on short allowance of flour—four pounds a day for seven men. (The full ration is 7 lbs 12 oz.) Our bacon is gone, & beans, & rice are scant; but coffee is in plenty and will outlast every other item. Our flour will hold out at this rate six days & those must bring us to the

Diamond River, or back to the crossing—the former if possible." As usual Gilbert had had no time for geologic investigation, except to note that the "granite cliff continues to show much schistose rock in gneiss, chlorite slate &c" and the basalt veins, as he supposed them to be (having "no time to examine them") had appeared at "3 or 4" points.[14]

On October 17, Gilbert reported that there was, "No change in the features of landscape or geol[ogic] formation" during the day's coverage of three and a quarter miles. The eighteenth was "another day of the same sort," geologically speaking; miles covered also the same. "Tomorrow morning," said Gilbert, "Roberts & Hecox are to start ahead for Diamond R. following the first bench 900–1000" feet above the river. "They carry a demand for grub."[15]

While waiting for the boats to be repaired on the morning of the nineteenth, Gilbert illustrated his notes with a sketch:

> Here for the first time I see our Indian Mitiwara dress his hair. The hair is cut square across in front so as to just shade his eyes. Behind[,] it hangs to the middle of the back & is loosely twisted in a dozen ringlets. To dress it, he covers it all with soft mud—parts it behind so that the long part hangs forward over his bowed head in two ropes. These he twists slightly & wraps turbanwise around his head. The front lock is then brushed up and adheres to the turban, giving a Ciceronian appearance if I remember rightly the bust of Cicero. It is said (I know not how truly) that this is done to kill lice. Our boatmen practiced it every two or three days. When the mud had dried it was rubbed out. The ordinary wearing of the hair is in a loose queue behind with a band near the end, while the front hair hangs straight to the eyebrows.[16] [At 10 o'clock the boats left camp.]
>
> At noon, we found a salmon [Colorado Squawfish] attached to a line & pole & hooks & two pieces of Bacon—all of which gave us assurance that we had not far to go. A little later we found a float from Hecox announcing D[iamond] R[iver] 6 miles from our last night's camp.
>
> By pushing we made D. R. at nightfall.
>
> The character of the Cañon immediately on the river has changed in great measure. The plutonic metamorphic cliff has become less steep and softer. The shore of the river can be traveled on foot if one is willing to climb 50 or 75 feet occasionally. . . . The water surface is broader & the rapids shallower. Just below D. R. is a long rapid of course, but the slack water above is not of great extent. The current has been so swift today that we have had to row the boats most of the way.

On the twentieth, Gilbert "lay in camp at Diamond River all day resting or trying to. The river trip has proved very exhausting," he said, "& after 24 hours of nothing to do . . . I still feel as though just out of a threshing machine." Since leaving Fort Mojave, the boat crews had passed 208 rapids and covered 222 miles.[17]

Wheeler's Colorado River exploit failed to give him the favorable publicity he desired, and his surveys were soon forgotten. Years later they became of interest to the historians Richard Bartlett and William Goetzmann, who were writing about the better-known surveys of Clarence King, Ferdinand Vandeveer Hayden, and John Wesley Powell. In the absence of most of Wheeler's correspondence files, Bartlett and Goetzmann relied on what little could be found in western Americana archives and Wheeler's annual and final reports, principally volume 1.

By 1889 when volume 1 was published, Wheeler had spent almost a decade writing it, his difficulty with it perhaps reflecting his confused state of mind. Bartlett found Wheeler, who well knew that Gilbert named the Colorado Plateau, taking the credit, saying on one page that he had named it in 1868 and on another that he had named it in 1871. Such "discrepencies," said Bartlett, are "sprinkled" throughout Wheeler's work and "reflect something of the man's capacities."[18]

All of Wheeler's reports are to some extent misleading, partly because he had so much to cover up. Concerned here, as we are, with Wheeler's river trip up the Colorado, for which there are no words of unqualified support from Bartlett or from Frank Schubert (military historian for the Corps of Engineers) and very few from Goetzmann in his book *Exploration and Empire,*[19] the inconsistencies in Wheeler's volume 1 deserve further exposure.

Wheeler returned to Washington early in 1872 without the correspondence and notebooks that he had lost to the Colorado, but he had other sources to draw upon. He had access to the monthly reports he had sent to Humphreys, Gilbert's notes, and personal recollections of the men and officers who accompanied him.

Apropos the loss of his boat on October 11, he had written Humphreys on October 24, "The misfortune of swamping my own boat about 30 miles after the Canon was entered and the consequent loss of valuable public and general papers, notes, data &c, some of which cannot be replaced, was very discouraging at the time, while the attempt to push ahead from this point placed us upon half rations."[20] In volume 1, his phrasing of the incident disguises the fact that his own boat was the casualty.

In the letter to Humphreys, Wheeler added that the party's situation had looked serious, and indeed it did, partly because Wheeler had left the fishing gear with the land parties. But at any time from October 16 on, and perhaps before, the party could have left the river and walked along the mesa to Diamond River. Putting his men on half rations was justified, but Wheeler need not have identified his location on the sixteenth as "Starvation Camp," and he probably did not need to stand guard over the rations. In volume 1 he said that the "entire rations of the party scarcely made a re-enforce" to his "blanket pillow" and that, as of October 17, it had been for several days "necessary to guard the entire stock of rations in person."[21] If such were true, nothing in Gilbert's notes or in Wheeler's letter of the twenty-fourth to Humphreys confirms it.

Of the three historians who have dwelt most extensively with Wheeler in their writings, the criticism that best fits their composite response to what all three consider a fruitless endeavor comes from Frank Schubert in *Vanguard of Expansion*. He concluded that the "ascent of the Colorado . . . was superfluous," pointing out that Ives had taken his boat up the river to the head of navigation and that Powell had come all the way downstream from the Green. "Wheeler paid dearly for the unnecessary journey," said Schubert in referring to the losses caused by the boat disaster. "His impetuosity and publicity-consciousness seriously diminished the results of his first season's work."[22]

FOUR

Lyons and Wheeler Mining Company

WHEN WHEELER LEFT the Grand Canyon on October 19, he headed for Truxton Springs, where his land parties had their camp. There he reorganized the parties and sent them by different routes to rendezvous at Fort Whipple near Prescott, Arizona. The makeup of the parties was noted in his book of special orders along with the statement, "Special and detailed instructions will be furnished to the commanding officer of each party."[1] After Lieutenant Lockwood and his party, including Gilbert, reached Fort Whipple, where they spent several days between the second and sixth of November, Lockwood headed back to Mohave County, where he met Wheeler in the Hualapai Mountains (south of present-day Kingman). There were other members of Wheeler's parties who did likewise: John Koehler (or Kohler) and Frank R. Simonton from Lieutenant Lyle's party and Wheeler's brother Willard, whom he had placed in executive charge of "Main line No. 2." (Willard Wheeler generally served as a clerk.)

Wheeler with a small "side party" had left the Truxton camp on October 25, one day after the other parties. With him were two prospectors: E. Martin Smith, one of five assistant surveyors engaged in May,

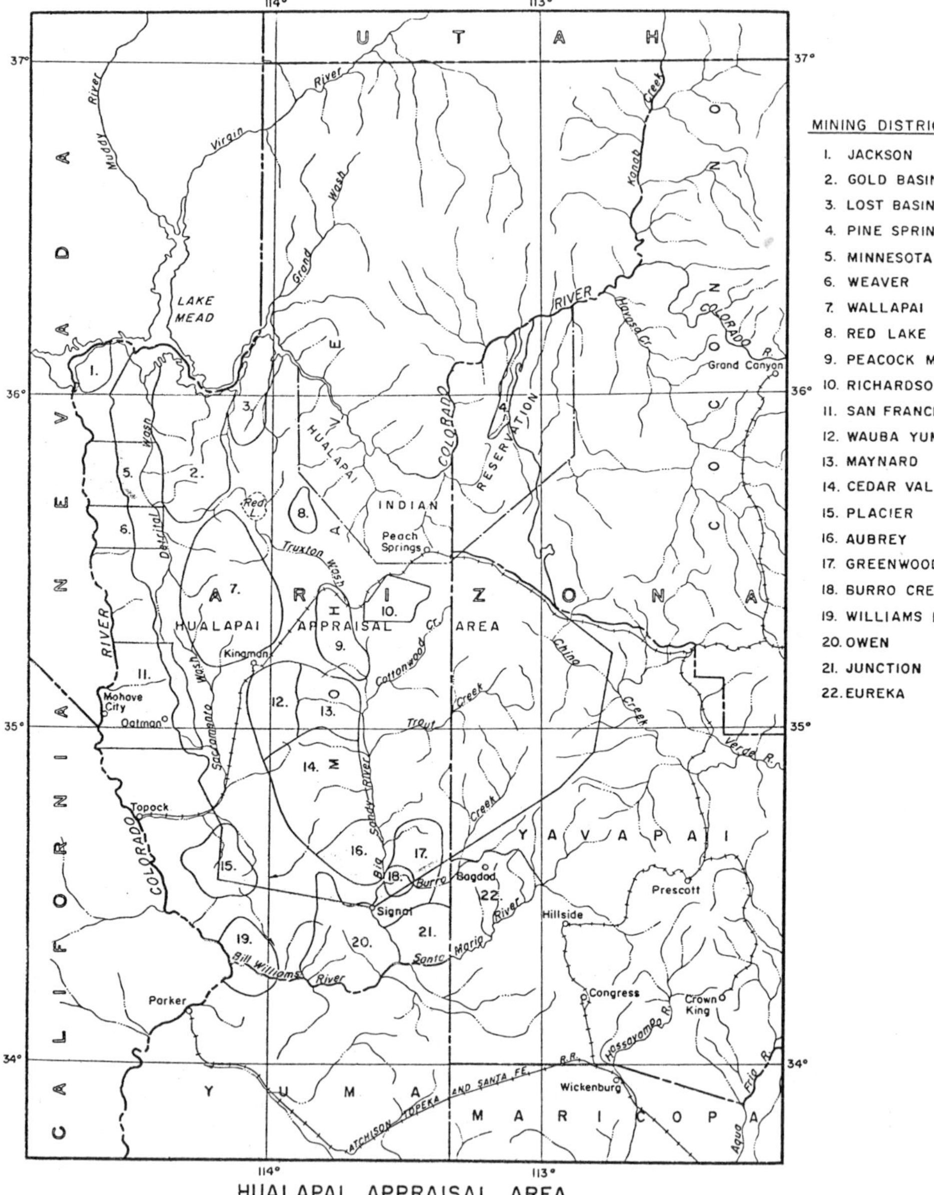

HUALAPAI APPRAISAL AREA
SHOWING
MINING DISTRICTS OF RECORD BY 1883
MOHAVE, YAVAPAI AND COCONINO COUNTIES, ARIZONA

SCALE 0 10 20 30 40 50 MILES

"Maynard Mining District, represented as No. 13, can be compared with Wheeler's map as to its general location in relation to Kingman (Beale Spring on Wheeler's map). Grapevine Creek on Wheeler's map is shown here as a broken line running through the middle of the district."

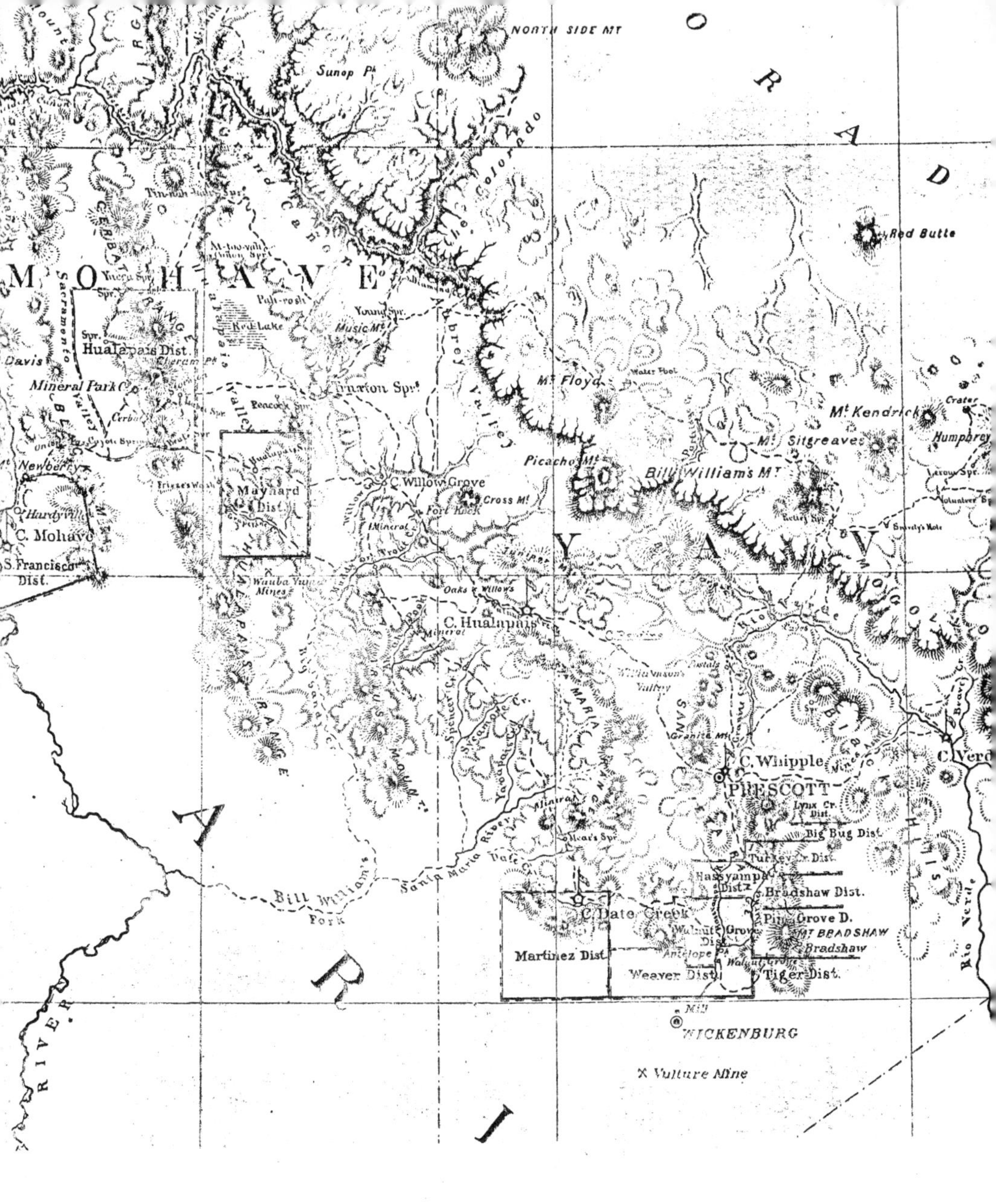

Maynard Mining District, as represented by George M. Wheeler
"Preliminary Report of Explorations in Nevada and Arizona [in 1871]"

Senate Executive Document 65, 42 Congress, 2nd Session [Serial 1479], 94.

now serving as guide, and William McGeary, engaged in May as one of twelve packers. En route to the Hualapai Mountains, the party visited a mining district or two before meeting Koehler, Simonton, and Willard Wheeler. On November 17 fifteen mining locations were made, and on November 18, fifteen more were made. Listed as "discoverers" were Geo. M. Wheeler, E. Martin Smith, and John Kohler. Coincidentally, on the eighteenth, the *Inyo Independent* posed the question, "Did the Government fit out a private prospecting expedition?"[2]

Aside from cooperating with California and Nevada mining entrepreneurs by supplying information useful to them—several prominent San Francisco businessmen are named on the mining locations—nothing was found to implicate the government in Wheeler's scheme. Nor did all his civilian assistants become involved in it. His artist, Edward M. Richardson, his principal scientists, and many other civilian assistants are not named on the location notices or on the conveyance deed to Lyons and Wheeler Mining Company, executed in Washington in February 1872 with the assistance of Senator William Morris Stewart.[3]

The *Independent* was in a fortunate location for keeping track of Wheeler, but even its informants such as Peter Monto, seem not to have known what was going on in Mohave County. So covertly did Wheeler operate and so remote were his mines that nothing appeared in the press to connect him with them until 1883 when a reporter for the *Mohave County Miner* happened upon the mining claims in the county's mining records and book of deeds. After mentioning that Wheeler had been in the county before to survey the Fort Mohave Indian Reservation—he had done so for General Ord in 1868—the *Miner* said:

> Lieut. Wheeler again visited this county in the fall of 1871 and camped for several days in the main wash running into the valley from the Wallapai mountains, which has since been called Wheeler's Wash. With his expedition . . . came also Major [sic] Wheeler, a brother of the Lieutenant, and a party of prospectors, who were outfitted by San Francisco capitalists, among whom were F. L. A. Pioche, Isaac Friedlander, A. J. Bowie, F. R. Simonton, Frank Soule and others whose names appear on the older locations made by this party. . . . Wheeler and his party at once proceeded to business on their arrival in Wheeler's Wash by building a house and forming a permanent camp which they christened "Bottle Camp," from the number of medicine bottles they had with them, we presume. They at once formed a new district under the name of *Maynard District,* adopted a set of bylaws and regulations and elected Francis Klett as Recorder. Among

> those who were present in the district at its formation the following are best known; viz: E. Martin Smith, Francis Klett, Lafayette Maynard, for whom the district was named, John Kohler, W[illiam] McGeary and D. W. Lockwood.[4]

Willard Wheeler, nine years older than George, was on the the survey payroll most of the time until about 1875. The title *Major* appears to have been a sobriquet. Francis Pioche was the wealthy importer and mining entrepreneur for whom Pioche, Nevada, was named. Isaac Friedlander was a commission merchant and bank director who was said to control "the wheat trade of California and the entire coast." He was called by a San Joaquin Valley newspaper the "most insatiable land grabber in the United States."[5] Augustus Bowie may have been the mining-engineer son of Augustus, Sr., a surgeon, but Augustus, Sr., was more likely to have the financial means to invest. Frank Simonton who prospected for Wheeler while serving as his assistant surveyor seems not to have been a San Francisco area resident. Frank Soule was editor of the San Francisco *Morning Call*. Lafayette Maynard was listed in San Francisco city directories as a "capitalist," as was Henry Lyons, Wheeler's partner in Lyons and Wheeler Mining Company, a California corporation based in San Francisco. McGeary, Smith, and Koehler (or Kohler) were familiar with Mohave County mining prospects before Wheeler hired them for the expedition. Klett, engaged in May as assistant surveyor, and Lieutenant Lockwood appear to have prospected in Mohave County while Wheeler was on the river.

Others among Wheeler's employees who signed powers of attorney "conveying to him the right to represent them in anything which might be found" were Frederick W. Loring, Wheeler's secretary; John Smith, assistant surveyor; Joseph R. Mauran and Charles E. Fellerer, assistant topographers; Louis Nell and Peter W. Hamel, chief topographers; Timothy O'Sullivan; Lt. David A. Lyle, executive officer; Thomas J. Gibson, William P. French, Asa Miles, Andrew Michell, George W. Evans, and Jacob Klinginschmidt, packers; Thomas F. Vance, blacksmith; Walter J. Hoffman and Adam H. Cochrane, acting assistant surgeons; Edward P. Austin, astronomical observer; Ferdinand (or Fred) Bischoff, collector of natural history; William J. Bradley, meteorologist; John Corless, chief packer; and William Ord. At least twenty of Wheeler's civilian assistants did not sign powers of attorney. Some of them may not have been invited, some may have felt that involvement was improper, and some may not have been interested in mining company investments.

The history of mining in the Hualapai Mountains of northern Arizona goes back to 1863, when John Moss of California and others began prospecting there. California newspapers reported so favorably on their finds that some twenty-five hundred locations were said to have been made there by 1866.[6] Such an influx of miners into the lands of the Hualapais created tensions that led to violence. In 1866 the friendly Chief Huaba-Yuma was murdered. In San Francisco the *Alta California*[7] called it an outrage—"one of those cowardly outrages which do more to provoke 'Indian atrocities' than all other causes combined." A month later Indian tribes from Hardyville on the Colorado all the way to Prescott were said by Arizona newspapers to be on the war path. Mining entrepreneurs feared for their investments, and miners for their lives. The War Department was beseeched for help. The department complied: Indians were to be confined on reservations in return for rations.

The primary cause of Indian depredations that led to killings was hunger, then rife among the Hualapais. Indians who were caught slaughtering a rancher's cattle often were summarily killed. So were others, such as Huaba-Yuma who had done nothing to antagonize the whites. Seldom did the Hualapais take revenge. Author Dennis Casebier in a relatively recent book wrote that it would be difficult to prove "that all the Hualpais together . . . had killed as many as 25 white men" prior to 1871; up to that time white men had killed at least 300 Hualpais, "perhaps . . . closer to 400."[8]

With the March 1871 arrival of Captain Thomas Byrne with Company F of the Twelfth Infantry to establish Camp Beale's Springs—the camp site is now part of Kingman—the depredations ceased. From this able leader, white troublemakers soon learned that the Hualapais also had rights. Byrne, said Casebier, strictly enforced his orders from General George Stoneman which were "observe a strict impartiality and whether he be citizen or Indian who is wronged, either shall equally claim and have protection."[9] The second influx of miners and ranchers was underway when Wheeler arrived in November without an escort. Before the year was out there would be about five hundred people in the Cerbat and Mineral Park mining towns near Camp Beale's Springs; in April one resident had counted only fourteen. Under Byrne, who made the Hualapais his friends, peace reigned.

Southeast of Camp Beale's Springs was Wheeler's camp, presumably on Grapevine Creek, which can be found on most maps of the region. Maynard Mining District is shown and described in Wheeler's report:

> This district was discovered in 1871, and lies on the eastern slope of the Hualapais Mountains, at a distance of thirty miles from the Needles on the Colorado River, and the railroad near the thirty-fifth parallel passes within nine miles of the principal locations. The mineral belt covers an area of nearly twenty square miles. The veins are similar to those in the Hualapais district, having the same direction, and in fact, to a remarkable degree, these districts are counterparts. No work done yet. Wood, timber, and water are plenty. The site for a mining-camp is very desirable. This locality also will act as a center, from which much prospecting will be done further down the same range; also to the south and east, and bordering the country of the Apache-Mohaves, from which locality float-material was noticed in different places.[10]

There was as yet no railroad, and there would not be one as far as Kingman until 1883. First called the Atlantic & Pacific and later the Santa Fe, it paralleled for a considerable distance the wagon road constructed during the late 1860s by Edward F. Beale. Most of the developed mines in Mohave County were in the northern part where towns had been established and stamp mills built. This Wheeler knew, but he was not to be deterred by the astronomical expense and inconvenience of moving ore a distance of eight to ten miles by pack train and then hauling it twenty-five miles or more to the nearest mill.

Soon after Wheeler returned to Washington, D.C., early in 1872, he prepared the necessary papers to form Lyons and Wheeler Mining Company. On March 18, with thirty-one powers of attorney and a deed dated February 14 in hand, he appeared with Senator Stewart before a notary public and transferred to the mining company the properties listed on the mining locations made in November 1871. Included was "the first South Extension of the Lyons Lode," which was in the senator's name, for he, too, had given Wheeler a power of attorney. The lodes and ledges identified in the deed were named for the participating parties in the venture, i.e., Wheeler Ledge, Willard Ledge, Kohler Ledge, Friedlander Lode, Maynard Lode, Pioche Lode, McGeary Lode, etc.

Not much is known about Wheeler's partner, Henry A. Lyons. San Francisco city directories show him as active in real estate and identify him as a "capitalist." From 1865 to 1870 he lived at Lick House, then the finest hotel in San Francisco; thereafter he moved to the Grand Hotel for two years, and then to a private residence. His office address was a few doors from 409 California Street, where Lyons and Wheeler Mining Company was located in 1873–74. Lafayette Maynard, who died in December 1876, had an office at that address for a year or two, and so did Willard Wheeler.[11]

The deed executed on March 18, 1872, conveyed not only mineral rights but also water rights and 1,280 acres of woodlands. It shows that 640 acres of woodlands were held by Willard Wheeler, E. Martin Smith, John Koehler, and William McGeary; the other 640 acres were held by Francis Klett, George Wheeler, E. Martin Smith, and Willard Wheeler. Certain lands with water rights "in and above Grapevine Creek" were held by Willard Wheeler, Smith, Klett, and McGeary; other lands and water rights "in and about Koehler's Springs" were held by Koehler, Smith, and George Wheeler. In addition the deed conveyed "all the right, title and interest . . . to the lands, waters and mines in said Maynard Mining District whether the same are hereinabove specially described or not."[12]

In 1872, McGeary discovered the Andrew Jackson Lode on February 28, and the American Flag Ledge on May 18, and on August 9, Koehler discovered the Emma Ledge. Among those holding interests in these discoveries were George and Willard Wheeler, McGeary, Smith, Kohler, Lockwood, and several of the San Francisco capitalists. The American Flag Ledge seems to have been the only productive property. However, it was discovered too late to be included in Wheeler's February 1872 deed. It was sold in 1877 to four Cornish miners for $25,000. Willard was last observed to be working at a mine in the general area during the spring of 1873. Soon afterward he returned to Wheeler's survey, where he was employed until 1875. McGeary occasionally was seen in Mohave County. The only person who frequently appeared in local newspapers was E. Martin Smith, who achieved success as a manager of mines for other companies. His association with Wheeler seems to have ceased after 1872.

Nothing was found by this author to indicate that any of Wheeler's mining associates benefited from their contributions to Lyons and Wheeler Mining Company, notwithstanding a thorough search for extant court records that might account for the lawsuits said to have contributed to Wheeler's destitute condition in his later years. On December 14, 1905, six months after Wheeler's death, his company was suspended "for not complying with statutory requirements."[13]

FIVE

West of the One Hundredth Meridian in 1872

THE FIRST YEAR THAT Wheeler was in charge of surveys west of the one hundredth meridian was 1872, not 1869, as he later claimed. The surveys of 1869 and 1871 were initiated by Gen. E. O. C. Ord, and they were not supposed to include more area than parts of Nevada and Arizona. Nor were they productive of the maps desired by the War Department. What Wheeler did produce there was information on mining districts that largely duplicated that contained in Rossiter Raymond's mining reports for the Treasury Department. Nevertheless, Wheeler felt confident that he had enough political and War Department support to be placed on a par with Clarence King, Ferdinand V. Hayden, and John Wesley Powell.

An undated report to Gen. A. A. Humphreys, apparently written by Wheeler in August 1871, states that "it is not presumed to be inconsistent to ask for an appropriation to be not less than one hundred thousand dollars" for the next fiscal year. Wheeler wished to examine "the great region adjacent to the areas of exploration already examined by parties" under his charge. In closing his five-page request he told Humphreys, "The mining question prolific of a great future, and now surrounded by imperfect methods for the introduction of capital and the proper development of properties, alone, affords a subject that to a person who seizes those needful points of practical Mining Industry may in immediate information seem to compensate for the expenditure requested."[1]

Neither in that request for funds nor in subsequent letters addressed to Humphreys during the winter of 1871–72 is there support for Wheeler's statement a decade later that during that winter he submitted a "plan for a systematic topographical survey of the United States west of the 100th Meridian."[2] His first semblance of a "systematic topographical" mapping plan did not appear until June 8, 1872, and it may have materialized only because of Humphreys's prodding. Humphreys's priority was mapping, not prospecting. On June 18, Humphreys asked the secretary of war to allocate seventy-five thousand dollars—not one hundred thousand—saying that the sum was "necessary" for the "early mapping of the region." Not only would it be of "great service" for "governmental purposes" but in furnishing the "information eagerly sought . . . by those interested in mining and other industrial pursuits."[3]

Although Wheeler had written Humphreys that it would be "wise and judicious to comprise in the scheme of the Exploration, reliable and minute examinations to be made at the most interesting localities," there is no evidence that his wish was communicated to Congress, which passed the act of June 10, 1872, directing the War Department to establish an astronomical base to assist in the acquisition of data essential to the making of maps.[4] That act provided for "geographical and geological" mapping surveys and constituted the first official reference to surveys west of the one hundredth meridian. Wheeler ignored the words geographical and geological when he designed his first letterhead, which reads, "Explorations, West of the 100th Meridian."[5]

That Humphreys was concerned that Wheeler begin fulfilling the intent of the act to map the public lands is evident in a subsequent communication from his office addressed to Wheeler by a subordinate: "The value of the results obtained at the astronomical stations will depend mainly upon the qualifications of the observers" and that the general desires "before you proceed to execute that part of the project, that you obtain his approval of the persons to have charge of the astronomical portions."[6] That eliminated some of the prospectors on Wheeler's payroll but not all. If Wheeler was irritated by such advice, for once he could not safely ignore it.

Wheeler knew that astronomical mensuration was an integral part of mapping. He was especially competent in that field but he had become too engrossed in mining exploration to concentrate on what should have had a higher priority. He was not immune to advice directed at the management of his explorations, and this is evident in the slower pace of the 1872 field season and the statements in letters to Humphreys regarding his supervision of personnel in charge of astronomical mensuration.[7] His work was greatly facilitated by Brigham Young's having made available the Mormon Observatory in Temple Square.

On July 13, 1872, from his rendezvous camp near Salt Lake City, Wheeler wrote Humphreys in detail his plans for the field season and asked for "an appropriation of ninety thousand dollars for the coming year." He promised that "hereafter more especial attention shall be directed to the elaboration of the astronomical portion."[8] Wheeler made various personnel changes in 1872. Some were required by the act of June 10, some by Humphreys, and some were based on the availability of officers and men. Lockwood and Lyle were replaced by the lieutenants W. L. Marshall and R. L. Hoxie; O'Sullivan, who was back with King, was replaced by William Bell of Philadelphia. (Bell should not be confused with the London doctor, William A. Bell, who had settled in Colorado Springs after doing photographic work for a railroad survey in 1867.) Nell was joined by John Weiss (both as chief topographers) and by Gilbert Thompson, hired as assistant topographer. G. K. Gilbert was back as chief geologist, joined by Edwin E. Howell as assistant geologist. Two scientists who later received wide recognition for their contributions to science—ornithologist Henry W. Henshaw and surgeon and natural scientist Henry Crecy Yarrow—joined Wheeler as collectors of natural history.[9]

William Bell had been chief photographer for the Army Medical Museum in Washington from 1865 to 1869. The excellence of his work was especially appreciated by Gilbert, who found photography indispensable in describing the characteristics of the steep escarpments common to the upper Colorado River region. "It is in the presentation of such subjects as these that the camera affords the greatest aid to the geologist," he said. "Only with infinite pains could the draughtsman give expression to the systematic heterogeneity of the material, and, at the same time, embody in his sketch the wonderfully convoluted surface, so suggestive of the folds of heavy drapery."[10]

Gilbert used the word "reconnaissance" when discussing Wheeler's surveys and complained of the number of miles he was expected to cover. Such conditions made photographs all the more important to a geologist, he said, for they enabled him to "restudy the view, of which a hurried visit [had] given him but a first impression."[11]

Wheeler had reservations about photography as a medium for illustrating his surveys. He would have preferred a painter; photography "assists us somewhat in gathering ideas of rock forms, but fails entirely to impress one with the grandeur of the shapes and details of coloring expressed in nature."[12] However, Wheeler was pleased with Bell's work as well as that of O'Sullivan, and he was especially impressed by Bell's successful use of the dry-plate process, then in the experimental stage.

Gilbert was often with Bell, especially during November. On November 6 he described Bell's dry-plate photographs which were taken between Kanab and Lee's Ferry. Some include views of the Paria River, which flowed through John Doyle Lee's ranch before joining the Colorado River; others are of the Colorado canyon.[13]

Usually Gilbert was with Hoxie's party; briefly he was with side parties led by an officer on loan from another branch of the army; sometimes he worked alone. During the first 130 days in the field he averaged 16.1 miles, 14.8 of them on mule. As a result of too much riding and not enough time for geologic study, his notes were not suited for a more lengthy treatment than that appearing in Wheeler's progress report. Gilbert was at his best in 1872 when he was writing about Mormons, their religious convictions, and their irrigation projects. "Dined by invitation with Mr. & Mrs. Lee (John Doyle)," he wrote in his journal on or about November 10. "The Dinner was a surprise—bountiful & well cooked. Mrs. Lee of 'Lonely Dell' is a black haired English woman of beauty & verve. The bright kerchief she wore on her head gave a gypsy-like appearance & the stories of her adventures with impudent Navajos coming to cross at the ferry are thrilling in the extreme. John D. fought his battles over again. His theory of Indian treatment is good, but is one of those things that are bound not to come to pass."[14]

Continuing the account of his visit, Gilbert described the premises: "The house of JDL has one low room & 10 inhabitants. It is half dug in the shale & half built of stone. Two wagons nearby serve as sleeping apartments. Before the door is a spring that flows from a steep slope of shale trod to mud by the cattle & devoid of vegetation. Back of it rises the Red Sandstone cliff & in front stretches the desert plain cut by the Colorado chasm. The largest tree is greasewood & *en fin* the picture is one of intense squalor & desolation. Imagination could not invent a more appropriate home for such an outcast."[15]

At Kanab on November 20, Gilbert called on Mrs. A. H. Thompson, whose husband was a member of Powell's survey. Powell had been doing geologic and ethnological research in southern Utah since 1870.[16] Thompson, his chief topographer, was in charge of mapping the region.

Wheeler's duplication of the efforts of Powell was not his first intrusion into areas of research to which civilian survey leaders had a prior claim, and it would not be his last. In 1871 he had sent the small party headed by Gilbert and O'Sullivan into an area of Nevada previously studied by King. Now he had Lt. W. A. Dinwiddie, to whom Gilbert had been briefly assigned, and a main party under Lt. William Marshall invading a region where Powell had been working since 1870.

In Wheeler's progress report for 1872, he said that Marshall and Dinwiddie had "visited at special points the lower of the main grand cañons of the Colorado," points where there were river crossings as far up Glen Canyon as the Crossing of the Fathers (El Vado de los Padres).[17] In a letter to Humphreys dated October 16, he said that Marshall was to work around the heads of Kanab Creek, the Paria, Birch Creek, and Dirty Devil south as far as the Colorado and to examine all the Colorado River crossings used by "marauding bands of Indians" that visited the southern and eastern settlements in Utah. That assignment took Marshall as far as Hite, located on the right bank of the Colorado at the mouth of the Dirty Devil, a considerable distance of almost a hundred river miles upstream from the Crossing of the Fathers.[18] (After the construction of Glen Canyon Dam and the filling of Lake Powell, Hite was relocated.)

In the same letter, Wheeler said that Lieutenant Dinwiddie with a small party of one topographer, one geologist (Gilbert), one photographer, and a few pack mules was to visit the Grand Canyon and enter it at three separate points to obtain specified measurements in the rock strata, certain views, and geologic information.

Gilbert's notes for his examinations of Grand Canyon and vicinity are useful in determining the itinerary of the party and the specific locations of some of Bell's photographs.[19] The overlapping of Powell's study area by Dinwiddie and Marshall would later become a matter of serious concern to Congress. The act of June 10 did not discontinue the mapping programs of the other survey leaders, though Wheeler might have been happy if it had. Had he been perceptive of the act's stated intent he might have kept his self-interest in locating mining properties under better control.

Nothing travels faster than news of the finding of gold, no matter how little. A few traces were found in Glen Canyon in October 1871 by three men who were on the way to meet Powell with supplies when he disembarked from his second trip down the river.[20] The assignments of the Dinwiddie and Marshall parties in 1872 suggest that Wheeler had heard the news. Furthermore, E. Martin Smith, one of Wheeler's prospectors in 1871 and possibly still in his employ, also was in the Glen Canyon area. In mid-November, from the same general area, Gilbert said that Smith had "passed through here six weeks ago & reports that his party made strikes."[21] By then Wheeler was in Arizona at some unknown destination. In his progress report for 1872 he said that he and his parties had examined twenty-five mining districts in Utah, twelve in Nevada, and eleven in Arizona. The districts in Utah and Nevada are listed by name. The districts in Arizona are not.[22] The omission is suspicious.

SIX

1873: An Archival Anomaly

THE DEFINITIVE ARTICLE on the "dismembered" records of the Wheeler surveys was written in 1964 by C. E. Dewing, for many years an archivist at the National Archives. On December 16, 1929, the acting director of the U.S. Geological Survey (USGS) wrote the chief of the Army Corps of Engineers seeking transfer of Wheeler's records to the survey's office. Dewing thought they were largely intact when they were transferred, except for maps and photographs that had been "assimilated" into the corps's files, and several volumes of letters received and letters sent, especially those for 1873.

On February 12, 1930, USGS director George Otis Smith, having deemed Wheeler's records "useless," wrote the Interior Department secretary's office proposing that they be destroyed. Within a month, J. Franklin Jameson, on behalf of the librarian of Congress, wrote Smith to suggest that a western university might be willing to preserve them.[1]

On March 24, Smith wrote to the University of Utah, offering it the "one ton" of old records he wished to get rid of, explaining that Wheeler's "published report . . . probably presents all of the material in a form more convenient for reference than in the original notebook form." Despite the negative tone of Smith's letter, the university seemed eager to obtain the records. Negotiations were underway when it was discovered that the proper steps to donate them had not been taken. Smith asked the chief of the Army Corps of Engineers on July 21, to resume custody of them, and they ended up in a basement corridor of the Department of War.[2]

The next depository for Wheeler's "useless" records was Stanford University, where they were sent in January 1931 "under senatorial frank." In 1960, Stanford offered what had not been dispersed to other institutions or interested individuals to the National Archives.[3]

Whether Wheeler's 1873 folios of letters sent and letters received were missing because someone had destroyed them or whether Wheeler had taken them home to work on and failed to return them to his office is not known. To write this chapter, it has been necessary to rely mainly on Wheeler's 1872 and 1874 records, copies of his correspondence found in other War Department files, Interior Department files, and the journal of artist A. H. Wyant, who accompanied one of Wheeler's parties for a two-month period.

On July 13, 1872, Wheeler requested Humphreys to obtain $90,000 for the 1873 season. In supporting his request, he said in part that no other department of the government had the facilities to do the explorations equal to those of the War Department, which had been doing them "since the administration of President Jefferson, who sent out Lewis and Clark."[4] Apropos the requirements of the June 10 act to provide data for the making of maps, he promised to direct "more especial attention" to the "elaboration of the astronomical portion."[5]

Wheeler may have heard that Hayden planned to work in Colorado in 1873 and sought to preempt him with a letter to Humphreys dated February 3, a copy of which was found in War Department files. However, Hayden had written Interior secretary Delano on January 17 for approval to work there, and this had been obtained.[6] Wheeler's letter to Humphreys stated that one of Wheeler's parties would "enter certain portions of the area between Denver, Colorado, and Prescott, Arizona." He added that someday Congress and the public would see the advantage of "surveys conducted with an efficient organization and centralized under one chief and executive head."[7] Wheeler's goal was to have the civilian-led surveys consolidated under his leadership.

In May, Wheeler sent Lieutenant Marshall to Denver to head Main Field Party No. 3, the "Colorado Party," and Lieutenant Hoxie to Salt Lake City to head Main Field Party No. 2. In June, Wheeler went to Santa Fe, New Mexico, to coordinate the work of his parties and to direct the movements of Main Field Parties Nos. 1 and 4. He put Lieutenant A. H. Russell of the Third U.S. Cavalry in charge of one division of Party No. 1 and civilian assistant Francis Klett in charge of the other division. Klett, it will be recalled, was involved in Wheeler's mining scheme and served as recorder when Maynard Mining District was organized in November 1871. In 1873 he was Wheeler's personal secretary. He appears to have conducted his division in an orderly and circumspect manner.

In Santa Fe on June 20, Wheeler advised Humphreys that he had put Timothy O'Sullivan in "Executive charge of Party No. 4."[8] Attached to that party but traveling separately was topographer Louis Nell and his crew.

It may be that Wheeler was ordered by Humphreys at a subsequent date to remove O'Sullivan from command of Party No. 4, for Wheeler in his annual report named an officer as in command. Another view is that Wheeler or his superiors or both did not wish the annual report to reflect that Wheeler had a civilian assistant in charge of a main field party. Whatever the circumstances, O'Sullivan was in executive charge of a party, he was requisitioned about the same number of mules as the other parties, and he turned in the same number at Fort Wingate in November.

Around September 8, O'Sullivan and his party began their last expedition of the season. The photographs he took are mainly of Canyon de Chelly, the Paria River at Lee's Ferry, and Glen Canyon above Lee's Ferry. (There are a number of photographs at the National Archives that have not been identified, but they are more likely to have been taken in 1874 than in 1873.)

The rather large number of photographs taken of the Paria River and Glen Canyon region suggests their purpose may have been to pinpoint the most promising gold-mining sites. Although we do not know whether the collector of natural history in O'Sullivan's party also was a prospector, through G. K. Gilbert's journal we know that E. Martin Smith, who was on Wheeler's payroll in 1871, found gold in this area in 1872 and may have brought it to Wheeler's attention. Through Wyant's journal we know that O'Sullivan and his party worked in the general area for over a week in October 1873 before beginning the search for the San Juan crossing. So evasive was Wheeler about this part of Main Field Party No. 4's operations that one is inclined to wonder if it was part of his hidden agenda to locate gold mining sites in the vicinity.

From Wyant's journal and Nell's topographic data, one can follow the progress of the two divisions of Party No. 4. Nell moved with impressive speed. He left Fort Wingate for Canyon de Chelly on August 5, arriving there on August 8; O'Sullivan did not arrive at Fort Wingate until August 30 and finally reached Canyon de Chelly about September 18. Nell used an upper crossing of the San Juan and was working in Colorado by August 14. O'Sullivan left de Chelly for Lee's Ferry on September 25, arrived about October 5, and left on the fourteenth to search for the lower crossing of the San Juan referred to in Wyant's journal.

Wheeler was back to his fast pace in 1873, pushing his parties to survey almost as many square miles as they had in 1871. He claimed 72,500.[9] Nell's mileage figures would have been included in the total, but Wyant's probably were not. What Wheeler expected to do with mileage figures recorded by Wyant and the rough sketches of rock formations he made is not known. The journal appears to have been lost in transit to New York City along with the finished sketches Wyant expected to use in painting Canyon de Chelly and perhaps other scenic views. The sketches have not been recovered. When the journal was offered for sale in 1976, it was acquired by the University of Northern Arizona.[10]

Wyant's employment status, unlike that of Wheeler's artist in 1871, is ambiguous. Without official authorization to employ an artist, Wheeler had engaged Edward M. Richardson as an assistant surveyor. Wheeler's reports show Richardson as the survey's artist as well as an assistant surveyor. Wyant is shown only as the survey's artist. However, vouchers for Wyant's two months of service listed him as a laborer. It is not likely that Wyant, prominent and successful as he was, agreed to work as a laborer,[11] but he may have agreed to serve as an odometer recorder, judging from the data in his journal. Without Wheeler's 1873 correspondence it is impossible to say with certainty what arrangements were made for Wyant's services. From what has been said in biographical dictionaries and other published accounts, Wyant expected to be with a party under the command of an officer, certainly not a party commanded by a civilian reported by some of those sources to be a "brutal man."[12] Reassignments of officers and men were made as Wheeler deemed necessary, often occasioned by a party's failure to report at a particular post on schedule. For just such a reason, it may have been expedient to assign Wyant to O'Sullivan's party.

Wyant can be described as a reflective, quietly congenial person who, like Gilbert, tended to express himself in letters and journals. Photographs show them as tall, slim, and self-assured. Neither was a stranger to outdoor work, especially Wyant who grew up on a farm near Defiance, Ohio. O'Sullivan was congenial but otherwise their opposite. Reported to be small in stature, he also had a tendency to show off. Gilbert did not seem to mind this trait, nor O'Sullivan's profanity, but Wyant did. When O'Sullivan was with King, a member of that survey had written a friend saying that "one would think he had slept with Grant and Meade and was the direct confidant of Stanton."[13]

Wyant did not care for rough talk and uncouth behavior, and this became evident when he left Fort Wingate with four or five privates from the army, supplied to Wheeler by the War Department. "After eight days delay in Ft Wingate," wrote Wyant, "I left for Fort Defiance with a part of O'Sullivan's party, that part which was least fitted by their habits for civilized society."[14] Though he soon recovered from his initial shock, adjusting to reality like a seasoned soldier, the first few days were fraught with difficulties that would have been upsetting to almost anyone.

O'Sullivan had sent this small party out with one wagon and some mules at 8 P.M. Five men, including Wyant were on mules. At Stinking Springs it was discovered that Wyant's overcoat and sketching bag had fallen off the wagon during the night. The driver of the wagon took Wyant's mule to look for it, going all the way to the post. The sketching bag had been run over, "utterly demolishing" Wyant's drawing board and his bottle of whiskey.[15]

The next day the check mule fell sick, causing a delay that was complicated by heavy rainfall. Wyant said that they "ate & slept in a pouring rain" and in the morning they ate their breakfast in the rain. Without the check mule the other mules would not "budge the load" until the men had emptied the wagon; with a man riding "each near mule" on the left side of the team they got the team to move. After reloading the wagon, they traveled to Fort Defiance, where they were to meet O'Sullivan. Wyant referred to the Navajo Indian agent there—William F. M. Arny who had been appointed in June—as the "governor" and said that he was "very obliging."

The day-to-day reporting by Wyant, of which excerpts follow, is comparable to Wheeler's reporting in 1869. (Regrettably Wheeler did not follow that practice in subsequent reports, depriving historians of a rich source of data relevant to the surveying of the West).

On September 17, a reunited O'Sullivan party and twenty-four mules left Fort Defiance for Canyon de Chelly. Wyant busied himself with compass and odometer, jotting down miles traveled in each direction as they followed the trail to the brink of the canyon's southern entrance, a tributary of Chinle Wash.

Wyant reported on September 22, that they had spent three days in the center of the canyon. He making sketches; O'Sullivan took photographs. (Wheeler later published a portfolio of photographs taken during his surveys from 1871 through 1873. Included are O'Sullivan's incomparable view of Camp Beauty and those of other Canyon de Chelly scenes.)

On the twenty-third, Wyant "made a little pencil sketch" of what is now known as White House Ruin, then a ruin without a name. O'Sullivan not only photographed it but arranged with one of the party to take some shots of himself with John W. Conway, a Santa Fe packer in Wheeler's employ, and George M. Keasby, employed as a collector of natural history, after they had climbed to the entrance of the ruin. Their ascent was facilitated, said Wyant, by a "fishing line which was cast around a pole put there by the navajos, & thus a rope was drawn up by which [they] ascended to the abode of the witch,—a navajo character."[16] (The names of the three men in the photograph were not known until the recent discovery of Wyant's journal.)

A few days, later the party picked up Lee's Ferry trail. Still in Navajo country, a horse belonging to their Mexican packer was stolen. Wyant said, "Got up this morning to find that the noble Indians had stolen our bell horse. So instead of making an early start to where our mules can get grass we have had to wait till the conscience of the thief could be touched by a small sum of money." Wyant was fascinated with the process by which the horse was recovered and drew a diagram. Since daylight, he said, the packer had been looking for tracks that matched those of his horse. After he found them, Jo, the Indian guide, and another well-mounted Navajo "started out to determine that the trail took a course, then as fast as their horses could run they kept one on each side of that trail, & that too in a broad valley full of paths & horse tracks" until they caught up with the thief.[17]

On or about September 30 at Blue Canyon, or Dot Klish as it was called by the Navajo, the party was treated by Navajo to corn and watermelons. Wyant said that they ate watermelons until their "appetites for melon were exhausted." The following day, as they neared the Moenkopi farms of the Hopi, they came upon Indian tracks. O'Sullivan had them polish up and load their guns, a precaution that caused Wyant to chuckle when they found themselves among the friendly "Moqui." He noted in his journal their "fine spring, a good garden, plenty of melons, & [a] potato garden."[18] They were Oraibi Hopi, most of them running daily the considerable distance from their homes atop Third Mesa to tend their crops along Moenkopi Wash.

Upon leaving the Hopi, the party picked up the Mormon Wagon Road and traveled to Lee's Ferry, arriving about October 5.[19] It was a historic time to be there. Since December 1871 John Doyle Lee had spent much of his time establishing ferry service and developing a ranch on the Paria River a short distance above its confluence with the Colorado River. While building the first ferryboat, he used the *Nellie Powell,* Powell's abandoned boat, to cross the river.

By January 1873 Lee had *The Colorado* in operation at the site later known as the first upper ferry crossing. In April he developed a lower ferry crossing a half mile or so below the mouth of the Paria. In May *The Colorado* broke loose during a storm and was destroyed when it entered Marble Canyon. John L. Blythe built the next ferry boat and had it in operation by October at a site about a quarter mile above the first upper crossing. The approaches along the left bank were extremely hazardous, making it desirable to cross at the lower site when the flow of the river permitted.[20] (The remnants of the road to the upper ferry are still discernible but presently unsafe in places even for foot travel.)

As traffic picked up at the ferry, Lee was less often seen there. (In 1877 he was executed for his involvment in the Mountain Meadows Massacre in 1857, when Mormons and Indians ambushed a wagon train and killed over one hundred westbound travelers.) During his absence, the ferry was operated by Emma Lee, his seventeenth wife. Nothing in Wyant's notes suggests Lee's presence there from October 5 to 14. During that period O'Sullivan photographed the Paria River where it flowed across Lee's ranch and at other points. One photograph, too dark for reproduction, shows Wyant at his easel. It bears the caption "Looking down from the mouth of Paria Creek." The camp is on a bluff above the Paria. A covered wagon resembling the kind survey parties used and other appurtenances of a camp complete this historic scene.[21]

O'Sullivan took a number of views of the Paria, but whether he took views of the Colorado in Glen Canyon at the sites his titles imply is open to conjecture. With those sites now at the bottom of Lake Powell there is no way to authenticate such captions as "Cañon of the Colorado River, Utah, 25 ms above mouth of Paria Creek near El Vado de los Padres" or "Cañon of the Colorado River, near mouth of San Juan River, Arizona." The latter was in Utah, not Arizona, and it was thirty-five miles above the mouth of the Paria. The mouth of the San Juan was about 70 miles above the mouth of the Paria, a considerable distance to have covered and returned in time to leave Lee's Ferry on October 14. (Lake Powell is 180 miles in length, extending to the vicinity of Hite, Utah; its San Juan arm extends almost to Oljeto Wash.)[22]

After Lee's Ferry began operating, the hazardous "Crossing of the Fathers," sometimes referred to as Ute Crossing, was no longer in use by wagon travelers. It was, however, of interest to Wheeler, and in 1872 he had sent Lieutenant Marshall's party to work there. A sketch of the ford was drawn by Marshall's topographer and later shown in Wheeler's final report. Had O'Sullivan reached the ford, he would have thought it sufficiently important to photograph.

By 1873 Wheeler was interested in San Juan River crossings used by Indians and miners, for he was looking for a more direct route to the mineral-rich San Juan Mountains in Colorado and Utah. They were accessible from where topographer Nell and his party crossed in New Mexico and at other river crossings in that vicinity, but Wheeler wanted a crossing where the San Juan ran through the canyon. O'Sullivan and his party were sent to find a lower crossing, then known mainly to the Navajo and the Ute.

The San Juan Canyon, before the filling of Lake Powell, was 133 miles in length, with one crossing in its upper reach, now spanned by a bridge to Mexican Hat. In 1873 the crossing was a ford, later shown on maps as Navajo Ford. Wyant referred to it as the lower crossing, which it was, but the party failed to locate the trail that led there, or burdened as it may have been with a surveyor's wagon, O'Sullivan chose to seek another route.

The trail that once was in use to the ford from Lee's Ferry is described in a 1965 report for the National Park Service by C. Gregory Crampton and W. L. Rusho. Never more than a pack animal trail, it left the Colorado about a mile and a quarter above the upper ferry. Ascending a "huge sand slope," it circled the Echo Peaks on the eastern side, after which it led to Navajo Ford. By 1910 it was known as the "Buzzard's High Line."[23]

Upon leaving their camp at the mouth of the Paria for whatever vicissitudes awaited them, Wyant drew a little sketch in his journal which he captioned, "Concluding line across from Mrs. Lee's made on mule back 14th Oct. '73 [a]s we were leaving Peria [*sic*] creek for the San Juan." Recrossing the ferry they "went seven miles to a spring." On October 15 Wyant reported, "Train so broken down that we could only make 12 ms to an alkaline spring. Threw away part of the cargo."[24] For the next two weeks, they would find few places to camp where there was sufficient water, wood, and grass.

On the seventeenth Wyant wrote that the "party pushed ahead til 2 hours after dark for water but made a dry camp." His mule was "fagged out by 3 P.M.," so he "remained behind with Conway the packer, who was whipping in the 'played out.' " Worse was to follow: "He & I encamped under the most ample of all canopies—that of Heaven—with no food & no water & no thanksgiving in our hearts. We had only our saddle blankets & almost died of the piercing cold wind. Sage brush burns well & we built up a little fire & there was good grass for the mules."[25]

Reporting on their plight between October 18 and 22, Wyant filled several pages of his journal:

> After two hours trudging through sand we joined the party. When we came in, the guide, the country & exploring expeditions, & everything relating to either was being cursed. Poor Jose & Williams & I started ahead for Sierra Blanca—a crest on the high mesa—of white sand stone, in which there [was a] crater shaped basin holding plenty of sweet cold rain water. Williams filled some canteens—after filling himself—& went back to meet the party. After watering the animals the navajo went to make himself a pair of drawers out of a cotton flour sack—O'Sullivan the same day gave him an old pair of pants which were a great delight to him, & which being dark echo his black hair in a way to make a picture of him—while I lay down in the sunshine to get the frost of the last night taken out of me—with my head in a shadow of a sage brush. I suppose I went to sleep at once. Was awakened by the order to get clubs & keep the mules—packs & all—from pushing into the water hole where some must have been drowned. They were afterward taken down in an orderly manner two at the time. We rested there until seven in the evening, then travelled til nearly 11 P.M. losing the trail twice on account of rock over which we passed, & finally among plenty of grass & wood we stopped to herd our animals til daylight.
>
> To have no professional herder, & an insufficient escort—then to warm your feet nicely & roll yourself up in your blankets, to be kept awake by loud talking, swearing, & swagger, & splitting of wood to keep the pot of beans boiling thro the night; finally after radiating heat enough to drive the frost out [of] your blankets, you go to sleep perhaps at 10 or later—To be called at 11:30 that you & private Tinsdale may herd mules til 1:30 in the dark up & down hills, aroyas, cañons—through acres of fragmentary, angular rock, & the awful thorns of the cactus here and

yonder, [and] you cant tell exactly where a ledge or cañon wall [is] over which you had better not walk, to be expected to report to your successors at 1:30 A.M. that a lot of unruly mules—not used to be[ing] herded—are 'all right, 24 mules and 1 horse' & get in an hour late because all the little ridges & valleys are alike in the dark, find the fire out, hop-skip-&-jump into bed half frozen after trying to drink a small lump of ice which had been formed in your canteen in the meantime; not being able to sleep because your feet are stubbornly cold & refuse to be comforted until at half past three or four A.M. you hear some one call the packers, & from then till the mules are driven in [in] 30 minutes you have time to try & sleep. In come the mules—two or five missing—the packers swearing & calling the cooks as if that would bring in any number of mules. The cooks in their turn wished every d————d mule in the outfit was lost & they back to the post. The jaws wag, the kettles rattle & in an hour more you are invited to get out of bed & come to breakfast.

Next A.M. at 8 we were off again & made 24 ms to an indian ranch where I was forgotten in putting on the guard, & I reckoned on a good sleep, the first for some time. But the ways of Providence are inscrutable. About 1 A.M. I was awakened by a most unearthly yell. Our camp was in the middle of, & across a narrow part of a small cañon. This was done partly to keep the herd in the upper end where the grazing was good. Twice before they were frightened, but this awful yell was caused by their stampeding through & across our camp sailing like spectres across the small fire that was still burning, stretching across packs saddles beds & all like so many coursers. Getting up in the cold, putting on boots & overcoats, seizing pistols & carbines & swearing at the Indians for the little joke, we went in search of mules.[26]

Wyant's descriptive prose ranks with some of the best in the reports of the Corps of Engineers and the Corps of Topographical Engineers. Moreover, Wyant did not say an unkind word about any of the persons named in his journal. Rather he was quick to point up an unselfish act, whether that of a private or a civilian assistant. He found packer John Conway particularly companionable. When he griped about his plight, as others did theirs, it was with sufficient reason. A journal entry for October 23 reads, "Here it is nearly sunset & we're making a dry camp this side of the river still. This is the 10th day and we were to do it in four—There are no disgusted persons about our camp. O-no!" During the next few days, the guide repeatedly failed to find a trail that led to the ford.

By the twenty-fourth the mules had been fifty hours without water and the party's guide had vanished. "The poor devil's tracks were seen by us later in the day as we were on our way back to a second dry camp," said Wyant. The finding by Conway and Williams of "a small hole of rain water" cheered the party. Wyant wrote that notwithstanding their discomforts and there being no wood to cook with, they were then happier than they had been for hours.

On the twenty-fifth they headed back to Cañon Bonito, realizing that it was their only hope of survival. Wyant wrote, "It was awfully cloudy & hailed a little. Soon it snowed a little, then much & blew awfully, so that Conway and O'Sullivan had to keep ahead, & after making sure of the old trail, break it anew for us. We came to puddles of rain water near Bonito, & those mules with no water for nearly seventy hours danced around & licked up that water like so many dogs. Later we got in here in the snow which fell nearly all through the night. We are in a miner's camp & tolerably comfortable. Yesterday was the day on which we were to have been in Loma, nearly 200 Ms from here with a river running thro a Cañon lying between, with only one crossing for a hundred miles, & we dont know just where the crossing is, & we are on half rations, & soon we'll have none."[27]

O'Sullivan had given up the search by October 30, and the party headed for Chinle at the mouth of Canyon de Chelly. Wyant's journal entry for the thirty-first is typical of his readiness to express his approval of his associates. After mentioning the morning's breakfast of a "piece of bread" and a "pull" on his canteen, he wrote about Private Carroll who, "in herding the mules [had] got lost & knowing we'd find them on the morrow kept the animals 'bunched' closely, & allowed the others to sleep."

That night, "after a hard tramp of nine hours," the party encamped "at some delicious water. We all voted a full ration for supper, & for very plain food, none ever tasted better. Over the last of our coffee we lighted our pipes, & the piles of Sage brush which was to heat the sand on which we made down our beds—a little trick we learned from the Lee family.

In the morning Wyant wrote, "I've saddled my 'Jim' & turned him out to take another mouthful of grass before attacking the road. I think by tomorrow we will have completed a circle instead of gaining our objective point." And at noon: "Started out with Conway to explore—or confirm my impressions of yesterday that we were near the mouth of Cañon Dechelly. The landmarks though much disguised from being seen from another side I was certain of. So now C & I have just taken our luncheon—saved from our breakfast—within a mile & a half of our old camp at Musquito Pond. We are surrounded by navajos whom we've seen before & our mules are filling themselves with navajo corn fodder—The train will be up in a couple hours, when we'll go into camp for the night.

By November 4th the party was back at Fort Defiance. "We were well received by gov. Arney [*sic*]," said Wyant. "Once more we have plenty to eat." He also reported that Jo, the guide who deserted when he couldn't locate the San Juan crossing, put in his appearance in camp. Perhaps Jo, or Jose as he sometimes appears in Wyant's journal, hoped to get paid the dollar a day he had coming for his services up to the day of his desertion. Instead he was tied up. "Just what O'Sullivan will do with the poor devil I don't know," remarked Wyant, who then said with obvious relish: "Originally Jose—or One eyed Pete as he is known by at the post—got executive commander O.S. to hold his horse while he ran away. That is the best joke of the whole trip."[28]

Jose was not to remain tied for long: "Just as dinner was being dished up, the mexican packer—also [named] Jose—yelled out, 'Pedro, los indio.' All eyes were directed to the figure of our Jo who was going for life around the point of rocks within fifty yards of our kitchen fire. Half a dozen persons, S & K among the number, started in pursuit, but Jo was running for the higher stake, & won. Good-by Jo."

On November 5, the day before the party left for Fort Wingate, "the three distinguised"—Wyant, O'Sullivan, and Keasby—dined with Arny. Wyant reported a "good dinner of roast sirloin of Beef & a heart stuffed & baked. Potatoes mashed with cream, Squash—sweet as a yam, potato, Soup[?], Green corn—from the garden today, Beets, Cabbage, Sweet Butter, Strong Coffee & two pieces of Mince Pie." Afterward, O'Sullivan made "some tin types as a compliment to the family."[29]

As soon as Wyant reached Fort Wingate, Friday, November 7, at 2 P.M., and was comfortably housed with Lieutenant Samuel Fountain, acting assistant quartermaster, he wrote in his journal: "Must go at once & see about the chances of getting home by the first buckboard which goes out Monday 10th." Noticing a book on Fountain's table that he wanted to buy, he wrote down the title of John William Draper's *History of the Intellectual Development of Europe*. Then he wrote, "Am housed again with Mr. Fountain. Have a comfortable fire, a nice bed—a bath—invitations to breakfast, luncheon & dinner indefinitely & an offer of money to the amount of double my wants."[30]

Then there is a surprising development, perhaps significant to an understanding of the conduct of Wheeler's survey. The journal ends with a puzzling scrawl: "It was struck between day & dark." Wyant did not take the first buckboard out of Fort Wingate on November 10, as he had planned. Instead, for three weeks he was an invalid, cared for by his friends at the fort, his right arm paralyzed and "practically useless." The cause of the paralysis remains unknown because no record was kept at the fort's hospital. All we know is that Wyant returned to New York City early in December, spent most of 1874 regaining his strength and teaching his left hand to do what his right hand had done, and then took up where he left off on that day in August when he joined the Wheeler survey. Although for the rest of his life he was in pain, Wyant continued to create great paintings until he died in 1892.[31]

SEVEN

Of Mules and Men

WHEN O'SULLIVAN REACHED Fort Wingate on November 7, 1873, with his train of broken-down, mixed-brand mules, he learned that trouble was in store. Acting assistant quartermaster Samuel Warren Fountain refused to accept the mules because of their poor condition and also because very few of them were U.S. Army mules.[1]

The aftermath of this refusal presents more questions than answers, for the 27-year-old second lieutenant Fountain was soon relieved of his quartermaster duties and transferred to Fort McRae, New Mexico. Was his subsequent notification that he was to be court-martialed behind the transfer? Was it related to his refusal to accept O'Sullivan's mules? Or was it neither? The charges in the court-martial proceeding do not pertain to mules. To have brought such a charge was not possible, for Fountain had acted in accordance with his orders. What causes one to suspect the intent of the court martial is that it occurred after Fountain rejected O'Sullivan's mules and was subsequently required to accept them, apparently by a higher war department authority than the quartermaster department. Further, the court-martial hearing board refused to provide Fountain with the charges against him until a day or so before the hearing, leaving him no time to prepare for his defense.[2]

Fountain, fraught with worry because he could not obtain the charges and facing, as was inevitable, a setback to his military career, became so overwrought by November 1874 that he became ill. Meanwhile the case dragged on until December 1875. During that period, Major William

Redwood Price, whom Wheeler had known for several years, rounded up a few friendly witnesses among the ranchers and others who sold their products to the fort. Their complaints, petty and unsubtantiated, were put to rest by Fountain, who acted as his own attorney. With a free hand to run the fort, given him by his superior officer who was ill, Fountain may have exceeded his authority at times, but that was not proved during the trial. Nevertheless that charge against Fountain cost him a six-month suspension.[3]

O'Sullivan's mules may not have been the cause of Fountain's dilemma, but they certainly placed Wheeler in a touchy position. O'Sullivan's civilian status was all the Quartermaster Department needed in order to pounce, for ordinarily it was not expected that mules which had seen a season of western service would be in good condition, nor was it expected that all would be U.S. Army mules, and furthermore, O'Sullivan was not the only commander of a party who turned in broken-down, mixed-brand mules.

The genesis of the Quartermaster Department's action against Wheeler was Wheeler's practice of borrowing as many mules as he could from the department. What he couldn't borrow he purchased in the private sector, cutting into his appropriations. During March 1873 he asked Chief of Engineers Humphreys to arrange for the loan of "one hundred mules and five six-mule teams complete."[4] On July 30, he asked for authority to return 83 mules at the "close of the field season, at Military Posts nearest point of disbanding."[5]

Quartermaster General M. C. Meigs said he would be glad to aid the "Engineer Department" by accepting mules at such military posts as could use them but cautioned against turning in any that were "broken down and unserviceable." Meigs explained that the cost of feeding the mules to restore them to health cut deeply into the department's appropriation and that mules that could not be restored to health had to be sold as "unserviceable."[6]

Upon delivery of 72 mules to Fort Union, of which about 24 were O'Sullivan's, the depot quartermaster "examined them with the greatest care," and sent the following report to the chief quartermaster for the District of New Mexico in Santa Fe: number invoiced, 75; number delivered, 72; number lost and died en route, 3. Eleven were "broken down beyond recovery" and 55 were "expected to recover and become in time serviceable." Only 12 had U.S. Army brands.[7]

The investigation, initiated in Santa Fe, moved up the chain of command to Col. Stewart Van Vliet, Headquarters, Department of the

Missouri. From Fort Leavenworth, Kansas, on February 18, 1874, he wrote, "It will be observed that there have been some serious abuses on the part of some persons connected with the Wheeler Expedition . . . in regard to the mules turned over last Spring to that Expedition by the Quartermaster's Department, and it is recommended that a thorough investigation be had, as it is not understood how American Mules could be changed into Mexican mules in the course of a few months. It is presumed that some of the parties of the expedition were in charge of Citizens or irresponsible persons."[8]

Wheeler denied responsibility: "The question as to the condition of the mules I do not consider necessary to discuss inasmuch as it is not to be supposed that after a campaign of five to six months such as the nature of the expedition demands that animals would be in good condition, and furthermore their treatment or identity after having been turned in to the QM Dept cannot be established by any evidence within my control."[9]

The quartermaster general and the assistant adjutant general continued to pursue the matter only to have their investigation quashed when it reached the top. In mid-November 1874, from the secretary's office, came the following directive: "The Secy of War directs that these papers be filed with others previously considered. He does not wish to reopen this subject."[10]

For exactly one year Wheeler's mules had been the subject of controversy. Many time-consuming, paper-pushing hours had been expended before Secretary Belknap stopped the investigation. No investigation had followed the 1871 incidents of missing guides and murdered Indians and no investigation followed Wheeler's lack of good judgment in placing a civilian in charge of a main field party in 1873.

But Wheeler did not escape without a reprimand in the matter of mules. When in 1874 he asked Humphreys to obtain a "loan" of quartermaster mules for the approaching field season, the assistant adjutant general told Humphreys in July: "The Secretary desires you to instruct Lieutenant Wheeler that questions such as have arisen, and complaints such as have been made . . . must not again be a matter of annoyance to the Department, and that disagreements with Department Commanders should be avoided and their views received with that deference which the importance of their positions demand."[11]

Although Wheeler did not get the mules until July, they were not the only reason he was detained in Washington. During May he appeared at hearings he had instigated with assistance from the War Department with a view to getting the surveys of Hayden and Powell transferred to the department. Wheeler's letters to Humphreys since early in 1872 had urged that there should be only one major western survey and that it should be under the War Department. Humphreys had been noncommital, judging from the few extant letters that were copied for the files of other War Department offices. However, exchanges of letters among the secretary of war, President Grant, and the House Committee on Public Lands are supportive of a hearing to assess the merits of survey leadership under the War and Interior departments. Congress had for some time been hearing complaints about the duplication of efforts of the surveys and was especially interested in what that was costing the government.

In 1872 Wheeler had duplicated some of Powell's work in Utah, and in 1873 he had duplicated Hayden's work in Colorado, notwithstanding a prior warning from Hayden. The hearing record of the Committee on Public Lands shows that during the winter of 1872–73 Hayden told a military colleague of Wheeler's: "You can tell Wheeler that if he stirs a finger, or attempts to interfere with me or my survey in any way, I will utterly crush him—as I have enough congressional influence to do so, and will bring it all to bear."[12] (As it turned out, it was Powell's testimony before the committee that dealt Wheeler the blow that crushed him in 1879.)

Wheeler's resentment of Hayden was such that in Wheeler's testimony he questioned Hayden's fitness to head a survey. Committee member Herndon did not let that stand, saying: "You stated as your opinion inferentially . . . that Doctor Hayden did not have sufficient scientific information to conduct an exploring expedition of the character of that placed under his charge. What is your opinion on that point in regard to Mr. Powell? Do you think that he has sufficient skill and information to conduct one?" Hoisted on his own petard, Wheeler replied that he did "not wish to answer that question at all."[13]

The Public Lands Committee hearing on which Wheeler had placed his hopes was by that time turning against the very department that had sought it. The origin of the hearing is confirmed not only by extant correspondence but also by the committee chairman's opening statement: "As the War Department appears to take precedence in the matter, we will first call upon Lieut. Wheeler." Getting little of substance from Wheeler, the committee turned to Powell. Although no more experienced as a witness than Wheeler, Powell used his knowledge of up-to-date mapping techniques and his customary eloquence to great advantage, setting the stage for the consolidation of the surveys that materialized in 1879.

Richard Bartlett in his chapter on Wheeler's surveys surmised that passage of the Organic Act of March 1879 to consolidate the surveys may have been largely responsible for Wheeler's subsequent ill health.[14] Some of Wheeler's symptoms could be attributed to earlier developments. By 1874 he was having trouble with his own department. When he tried to get an officer of the corps to assist him in compromising the integrity of a geographer he wished to hire who had accepted an offer from Hayden, he failed; when he tried to get the Public Lands Committee to expunge from the record testimony given by the geographer relating to mapping techniques, he failed. Worse yet, Lyons and Wheeler Mining Company was failing, and the constraints placed upon his field operations prohibited him from working in areas where mining opportunities were more promising.[15]

Moreover, the committee's report did not relieve Wheeler of his anxieties about his future. Although it did not recommend that consolidation of the surveys be undertaken at that time, it said that when the day came, putting them "under the control and guidance of the Interior Department" would better serve the public interest.[16] As to operating costs, the report noted that the civilian-led surveys were being "conducted with less comparative expense than those under the War Department, considering the amount of money expended and the results thus far exhibited." The $90,000 Wheeler received in 1873, noted the committee, did not "embrace the expenses of the Army officers, the medical officers, nor of the sixty soldiers used as an escort." Powell's testimony that escorts were not needed had fallen on budget-minded ears. That and the committee's assertion that Wheeler's published work was "rather limited"[17] warned Wheeler that henceforth he would have to begin doing more with less.

On May 21, the day after the hearing ended, General Foster advised Wheeler that he was to have only $30,000 to finance the 1874 expedition; Wheeler had requested $95,000. Not one to readily let a superior interfere with his plans, Wheeler wrote Humphreys suggesting another source of funds, i.e., "the unexpended balances of the 'Appropriations for Surveys for Military Defenses' for the fiscal year ending June 30, 1873" that had been re-appropriated by Congress. "I have the honor," said Wheeler, "to suggest that an allotment from these balances of not less than $60,000 could be made to the work under my charge." Humphreys obtained the funds but cautioned Wheeler that he was to conduct his operation "with the greatest economy with a view to making as much progress as possible on the Topographical surveys during the season."[18]

Further encroachment on areas being surveyed by Interior Department parties was forbidden. Congress saw to that with the Sundry Civil Expenses Act of June 23. Nevertheless, Wheeler tried to enlist Humphreys's assistance in bypassing the act by getting the functions of his survey redefined. He maintained that there "need be no appreciable interference with any of the surveys . . . under existing laws" if his survey were defined thus: "to survey and delineate the surface and to investigate as to the resources of the public domain . . . West of the 100th meridian."[19]

Humphreys advised Wheeler on July 9, that any authority previously given him that conflicted with the act of June 23 was revoked, and on July 14, Humphreys advised Secretary of War William Belknap that Wheeler had been instructed to confine his operations for the present season to the area south of an east-west line "running through the highest of the Spanish Peaks, Colorado Territory, that being, apparently, the most southerly point reached by Prof. Hayden's Surveys." Further, Humphreys said, "Lieut. Wheeler has been prohibited, in express terms, from allowing any of his parties, or persons connected with his survey to make any surveys or examinations whatever north of the east and west line running through Spanish Peak," except to establish triangulation points to connect previous work and for ongoing work at the various astronomical stations. That left Wheeler a narrow band of land along the Colorado border lying south of the Spanish Peaks, all of New Mexico, six triangulation points outside the area, and the astronomical stations wherever work was under way for the collection of astronomical data.[20]

Added to Wheeler's woes in 1874 was the abrupt resignation of chief geologist G. K. Gilbert in June. On February 2, Wheeler had advised Gilbert, "You will be required to present your finished Report for 1871 and 1872 on or about April 1st and your complete Report for 1873 at as early a date subsequent thereto, as possible." Gilbert may have indicated he needed more time, for on the same day Wheeler advised, "You will submit a schedule plan for the final report upon the work in your charge, and render monthly reports of progress of such work until the time of final completion." Then, on February 14, Wheeler advised Gilbert: "You will submit as soon as possible a skeleton plan for the publication of a volume upon Geology, to be known as volume 4 of the finished reports. This plan should comprehend the number of chapters, chapter subjects, illustrations &c. including the results of the season of 1873."[21]

Gilbert remained on Wheeler's payroll through September, grinding out the required reports to Wheeler's specifications, but not entirely to his satisfaction. In discussing certain aspects of geologic investigations, Gilbert had alluded to and referenced studies by geologists in other surveys. On October 23, Wheeler advised him that he had "found it necessary in most cases to erase these."[22]

Wheeler's antipathy for civilian geologists by then was common knowledge. Gilbert's final report, which appeared in 1875, contained several deletions and changes made by Wheeler about which Gilbert did not remain silent, adding support to the conviction of civilian scientists that Congress should look to them, not to the corps, in matters such as mapping and scientific investigation.[23]

In addition to Gilbert's resignation in June 1874, another matter was coming to a head. On or about May 11, Wheeler had been interviewed about his mapping work by the New York *Tribune*. In mentioning the work of his predecessors, he had neglected to include Col. and Bvt. Maj. Gen. W. H. Emory. Emory wrote Wheeler a lengthy letter about the significance of his own work and questioned the propriety of Wheeler's having included in his eulogy some mappers whose work "consisted only of hasty sketches, without ever taking an observation of latitude and longitude or making any instrumental measurement whatever." Not receiving a response by June 12, Emory sent a copy of his letter to Wheeler to the *Tribune* where it was to be printed.[24]

Later than usual, a much-chastised Wheeler left Washington, D.C., to supervise the work of his field parties in the San Juan Basin, one of the few unrestricted areas open to him. Photographs of Pagosa Springs, Colorado, and archeological sites along the San Juan were taken by O'Sullivan. They are not as creative as one had come to expect from earlier work; perhaps O'Sullivan was inhibited by Wheeler's close supervision in 1874.[25] Like Wheeler, he was on a tight leash. Although their gross mistakes of the past were kept from public sight, their careers were coming to a close. O'Sullivan was thereafter relegated to darkroom processing of photographs and maps and could no longer go west to compete with his contemporaries in other surveys. Wheeler was restricted to mapping the West and no longer of much use to the mining entrepreneurs, who saved their favors for those who served them.

EIGHT

Sources: Primary, Secondary, and Suspicious

WHEELER'S BOOK OF orders, special orders, and circulars is a primary source covering the years 1871 through 1873. An entry, dated August 30, 1873, is a circular of several pages. It follows an entry dated December 27 and is preceded by a notation that it "should have been Copied in its proper place." Headed "In the Field," it contains disbanding instructions to officers, civilian assistants, and employees by name. Wheeler heads the list, stating he will leave Camp Apache about September 1, proceed via Salt Lake and San Francisco to Washington, D.C., and reach there about October 1.[1]

Occasionally Wheeler placed his order book in the hands of one or another of his executive officers, necessitating a delay in inserting a subsequent order of his own. The August 30 circular, however, may have been substituted for an earlier circular of that date. Because the circular is out of order and because neither O'Sullivan nor any of the members of his party are provided disbanding instructions in the circular, its authenticity should be questioned. It is altogether possible that Wheeler, finding himself in great difficulty after the disaster at Fort Wingate, had the circular revised to obscure his having placed a civilian in command of a field party from which a prominent artist returned with a paralyzed right arm.

Another of Wheeler's circulars, placed at the end of his 1873 orders and circulars, is undated. It reads, "Assistant T. H. O'Sullivan is hereby authorized to act as my agent for the purchase of the necessary Commissary Supplies for Civilian Assistants and employees as per Schedule allowance, to requisition for and receive forage for 25 QM mules and for such other army supplies at any point on his route as may be necessary to carry out the objectives of the party assigned to his charge."[2] Presumably this circular was issued by Wheeler in June to coincide with his letter of June 20 to Humphreys stating that topographer Nell was in charge of triangulation, and "Assistant T. H. O'Sullivan in Executive charge" of Party No. 4.

Although Wheeler later named an officer as leader of Party No. 4, O'Sullivan continued to conduct his own party much as he had earlier in the season. Without a copy of that circular, he could not have provided for the contingencies inherent in an expedition that required the purchase of supplies, the hiring of guides, and the replacement of broken-down mules. The missing date, in addition to the circular being out of place, afforded Wheeler an opportunity to withhold it from the view of a superior until he was ready for it to become a part of the record. We cannot know whether this was his intent.

In following O'Sullivan's trail from Santa Fe throughout the field season, dated vouchers for reimbursements might be useful. However, they were usually prepared in Washington months later, and O'Sullivan in the meantime had forgotten when and where he made his transactions. He was not one to be bothered with itemized bills-of-sale and receipts. A voucher dated September 29 states that on that day he purchased six hundred pounds of corn at 4 cents per pound and two seamless sacks at 50 cents each.[3] One would likely assume that a purchase of that size was made at an army post or a town. However, Wyant's journal for September 29 shows the party at Blue Canyon amid some Navajo, eating corn and watermelons. O'Sullivan may well have given the Navajo some money, but it is not likely that they sold him six hundred pounds of corn.

Another voucher shows that O'Sullivan paid Lee for ferry service the sum of $20 on October 30. Wyant's journal shows the party in camp near Chinle Wash on that day, having left Lee's Ferry on the fourteenth.[4] (As of April 1873, Lee had been charging 75 cents for "each

Horse & $3 for each" wagon.[5] Given the number of mules O'Sullivan had, he may have received a government rate.)

As we have seen, primary sources relating to Wheeler's survey operations are difficult to use, whether published or unpublished. Like his annual report for 1871, his 1873 report is misleading. Nowhere in the report is O'Sullivan credited with commanding a party of escort soldiers, packers, and civilian assistants—a party sufficiently large to require twenty-five mules. Readers of the report are informed only that "Mr. T. H. O'Sullivan, photographer, secured forty-two landscape views and one hundred and four stereoscopic views, a portion of which will be published."[6]

Only by implication does O'Sullivan appear elsewhere in the report. Under "Photographs" the report reads, "As heretofore, a photographer has accompanied the expedition, following a route from Santa Fe westward, via Fort Wingate; thence to Camp Apache, and the vicinity of the Sierra Blanca range, Arizona; thence northward, via old Fort Defiance, Moqui Pueblos, and the Cañons of the Colorado."[7] Except for the Moqui (Hopi) pueblos which O'Sullivan did not visit, his vouchers and photographs confirm that he worked at those places, but the dates on the vouchers may be inaccurate.

Another shortcoming of the 1873 report is the absence of any reference to the San Juan River search. Not only does Wyant's journal confirm that part of the assignment but a letter of instructions to O'Sullivan found with the Third Auditor's Accounts at the National Archives confirms it.[8]

Wyant's journal (unknown to exist before 1976 and subsequently published) and extant letters and memos at the National Archives raise questions that require revisions in historical references. For example, in Wheeler's 1873 report Wyant is passed off as an artist who "traveled with the photographic party, and made studies of some scenes in the Cañon de Chelle, one of which he proposes to put on canvas when his health will permit."[9] Wyant may have planned such a painting, for he wrote Wheeler in January 1874 asking Wheeler to send O'Sullivan's Canyon de Chelly photographs and inquiring about a valise of Wyant's that had been lost in transit between Santa Fe and New York.[10]

The tone of Wheeler's response does not indicate that Wheeler had at that time an interest in obtaining such a painting, much as he preferred color to the black-and-white renditions of his photographers. His response to Wyant reads: "Sir: Your letter of the 16th received. Mr. O'Sullivan will send you the photographs desired. I can tell you nothing of your valise. If you will send a full history of it will send tracer. Am gratified to learn that you are improving in health and hope that you may fully recover sooner than you expect."[11]

Wheeler's register and digests of letters received shows that Wyant complied on January 31, but the "Action" column does not show what if any action Wheeler took.[12] It may be that he wished to be free of any further association with Wyant. If so, he may not have expedited the tracer; and he may not have asked O'Sullivan to send the photographs. (It also may be that Wyant's sketches of Canyon de Chelly and Lee's Ferry were in the lost valise. Without them he was not likely to undertake related paintings.)

Art historians in particular are the beneficiaries of this new information. But caution must be used in dealing with Vouchers 13 and 14 referred to in Chapter 6 (n. 11). They purport to be "For Services as laborer" covering periods from September 1 to September 30, and October 1 to November 9, 1873, in sums totaling $138, and to be signed by Wyant on December 1 in Santa Fe. Wyant was briefly in Santa Fe on November 29 en route to New York City.[13] The vouchers leave historians in a quandary: If secondary sources written by art historians and art critics are correct, O'Sullivan may have forced Wyant to work as a laborer; Wyant clearly indicated in his journal that he felt imposed upon when O'Sullivan ordered him to herd mules and stand guard. If Wheeler—in order to obtain an artist who was at that time without funds to pay his own expenses—subsidized Wyant by putting him on the payroll as a laborer, that would account for the classification as such on the vouchers. However, Wyant expected to travel as the survey's artist as his contemporaries John F. Kensett, Albert Bierstadt, Worthington Whittredge, and Thomas Moran had for other western surveys. Neither Moran nor Wyant were physically strong. Whereas Moran's associates in the Hayden survey looked after his welfare, Wyant was not so fortunate. The most common comment made by art historians and critics regarding Wyant's western experience was that Wyant had joined the wrong survey.[14]

Wheeler's annual report for 1872 presents no such difficult problems for historians dealing with the western surveys. An artist did not accompany the survey, relieving Wheeler of the need to find a paid position such as he did for Edward M. Richardson in 1871 and Wyant in 1873. Wheeler's photographer in 1872 was William Bell, who could not be imposed upon with extra duties such as O'Sullivan had undertaken in 1871 and 1873. The self-assured and professionally established Bell performed only as a photographer. His western photographs did not immediately attract much attention, but lately they have greatly added to his reputation. Contemporary writers will find Wheeler's 1872 report and G. K. Gilbert's journal particularly informative on Bell's contribution to western photography.

Secondary sources vary in their treatment of Wheeler and his survey, especially biographical directories. Wheeler appears in a number of these directories, some compiled by military men. In some instances he may have written his own biographical sketch. An excerpt from an exceedingly long entry reads: "He has matured projects for the Astronomic, Geodetic, Topographic, Hypsometric and Cartographic field and office operations necessary for the complete Geographic Survey of the greatest accuracy of the whole U.S. after the most approved scientific methods."[15]

Another example is reminiscent of Wheeler's correspondence with Count von Moltke, with whom he associated in 1881 during his attendance at the Third International Congress and Exhibition in Venice. (Wheeler had been sent as the War Department's delegate to the Congress. There he hobnobbed with his kind, for in European countries, mapping was a function of military men, not civilian geologists.) The biographical entry states: "These surveys have received the approval and commendation of the highest authorities connected with the elaborate and most accurate physical surveys of Europe, including Field Marshal General the Count von Moltke."[16]

Wheeler was particularly hard on geologists in his report on the Third International Geographical Congress, going so far as to say, "The natural and necessary inferiority of all topography directed by geologists . . . arises from the condition that the inherent requirements of geological investigation demand more attention to the natural features of a given area." Parenthetically, he said that as a class they "are not capable or skilled in the exact or mathematical sciences that must be employed in the field observations and map construction."[17]

The use of Wheeler's reports requires considerable investigation of the underside of his operations. His reports are deceptive, as reports often are whether produced inside government or out. At least two historians have expressed their reservations about the use of government reports as primary sources.[18]

Nine

Government Science in Western Expansion

From the time of the Louisiana Purchase until the late 1860s, the Corps of Engineers reigned supreme in the field of government science in western exploration. Projects were carried out by civilian scientists under the direction and protection of the Corps of Topographical Engineers, and much progress in scientific investigation and mapping of unexplored regions was made.

Military involvement in science resulted from the needs of a young and largely unexplored nation. In 1802, even before President Jefferson saw the need to explore the region acquired by the Louisiana Purchase in 1803, he established the U.S. Military Academy, where the training of officers would include courses essential to topographic and scientific work. That Jefferson would be the one to establish a military academy at which he stationed a corps of engineers came as a surprise to his contemporaries, who had been urging the establishment of a national university such as existed in other countries.[1]

Frustrated in their efforts to get government assistance to establish a national university, its proponents sought assistance by another route.

In 1863, through the efforts of a congressman sympathetic to this goal, Congress was persuaded to approve the National Academy of Sciences as its advisory body on matters requiring scientific expertise. Because an appropriation was needed whenever scientific expertise was desired, the academy received little congressional funding until well into the twentieth century. However, an exception to this practice of neglect occurred in 1878.[2]

On June 20 Congress passed a sundry civil expenses bill that had a far-reaching effect. The act required the academy, at its next meeting, "to take into consideration the methods and expenses of conducting all surveys of a scientific character under the War or Interior Department, and the surveys of the Land Office, and to report to Congress . . . a plan for surveying and mapping the Territories of the United States on such general system as will, in their judgment, secure the best results at the least possible cost."[3]

The academy's acting president Othniel C. Marsh, professor of paleontology at Yale, set up a committee of like-minded colleagues called the Special Committee on Scientific Surveys. Among the committee's recommendations was consolidation of the surveys of Wheeler, Hayden, Powell, the Coast and Geodetic Survey (then under the Treasury Department), and the surveys being carried out by the Interior Department's General Land Office. The King and Lake surveys were not included, the first having been completed and the second nearing completion. The committee said that in order to "attain the desirable accuracy and economy, it is absolutely essential that there should be only one geodetic system, one topographical system, and one land-parceling system, all conducted under the same head"—the Department of the Interior.[4]

Although the committee recommended that "an independent organization"—the Geological Survey—be established within the Interior Department, it was not to be a mapping organization but a geologic one. The corps was to continue with such investigations and surveys as were "inseparably connected with engineering problems." Humphreys viewed the committee as stacked in favor of the geologists in the Interior Department surveys and complained bitterly at the hearings that followed. The corps got nothing new from the committee and lost something old, but it was not as deprived as it claimed to be. As an engineering department, its traditional role in time of peace included the improvement of rivers, harbors, and lakes to facilitate navigation; the reclamation of tidal lands to facilitate agriculture; the control of floods; and so forth. After the Civil War and well into the next century, there was more than enough work, perhaps too much, for the corps did little more than give lip service to the need, expressed by Congress during the next two decades, for irrigation and dam site investigations to assist in the settlement of the public lands.[5]

The year 1879 opened with civilian scientists seeking the support of their favorite congressmen. Perhaps no one of them was as influential in obtaining passage of the Organic Act of March 3 to consolidate the western surveys under the Interior Department as Abram S. Hewitt, a Democratic congressman from New York. Generally supportive of the corps in legislative matters, he could have been thinking of Wheeler when he said to his congressional colleagues that it was "not to be expected that the large body of scientific men required to make" the western surveys a success would "consent, willingly, to place themselves under the control of the younger officers of the Engineer Corps."[6]

The Organic Act was passed with little that was reminiscent of the academy committee's recommendations for reorganization. The act's provisions included an annual salary of six thousand dollars for the director of the Geological Survey; authority to examine the "geological structure, mineral resources, and products of the national domain"; and discontinuance of existing surveys—those of Wheeler, Hayden, and Powell—effective June 30, 1879. The public lands were to be classified "as arable, irrigable, timber, pasturage, swamp, coal, mineral lands" and other classes "as may be deemed proper." Congress had created a fact-finding agency that facilitated western expansion as well as enlarging the role of science in government.

Although the time had come when escort soldiers seldom were needed to protect field parties and a consolidation of the surveys was inevitable, it should not be thought that the officers of the corps had assimilated so little scientific knowledge that their expertise was no longer of any use in furthering western development.

Subjects taught at West Point, except those distinctly military, were much the same as those then being taught at the universities. Yale did not have a scientific school until the mid-1850s; the Massachusetts Institute of Technology followed in 1861. One might surmise that students with a scientific bent chose military service in the early years in order to qualify for West Point, especially if they could not afford a university. Like the science-oriented civilians who attended medical schools in the early years to get courses they needed, there was but one other alternative: study in Europe, preferably at Freiberg.

Some of those graduates from the military academy at West Point joined the Corps of Topographical Engineers before it was merged with the Corps of Engineers during the Civil War. Not only were they interested in the advancement of science but several were talented artists and writers. Captain James H. Simpson's report of his 1859 explorations for a wagon road from Camp Floyd, Utah, to Genoa, Nevada, comes quickly to mind for the excellence of his writing in describing the natural features of the land and the quality and scarcity of its waters.[7]

A decade earlier, Simpson, then a lieutenant, was in northwestern New Mexico at Chaco Canyon with Richard Kern, the party's artist. While Kern mapped and sketched, "Simpson moved delightedly from Chetro Ketl to Pueblo Bonito, then to Pueblo del Arroyo, visiting the accessible rooms, counting, measuring, and describing his discoveries."[8] To many of those "topogs," the unexplored West was a place to do postgraduate work. Together with civilian scientists, they combed the West for specimens of natural history while surveying it for maps and roads.

After the Civil War, with the Topographical Corps no longer in existence, Humphreys was without the manpower to continue the corps's western work. In 1867 Clarence King, with a letter of introduction to Humphreys from scientist William Brewer, presented to Humphreys a plan for a fortieth parallel survey. Such a survey would serve the interests of the private entrepreneurs who had been granted lands along the transcontinental railroad then in progress and the people who would populate farms and towns along the route. Furthermore, a survey financed by the War Department would enable the corps to regain its foothold in the West. Humphreys immediately approved the plan and placed escort soldiers at King's disposal. King selected his own survey crew and the War Department paid their salaries.[9]

King had attended Yale's Sheffield Scientific School, graduating in 1862. He met Brewer aboard a paddle wheeler plying the Sacramento River. Both were bound for San Francisco. For the next four years, King did exploratory work and mapping for the California Geological Survey. With James Gardner as his geographer, King was well qualified to do the fortieth parallel survey, and Humphreys was pleased with the results.

In 1866, following his graduation, Wheeler was assigned to the Army Corps of Engineers' San Francisco office. In a class of thirty-nine he had ranked first in philosophy and mathematics, second in engineering, and sixth in mineralogy and geology. His first meeting with Humphreys probably did not take place before February 1871, when he outlined his plan to survey public lands south of King's fortieth parallel surveys then underway. With King's survey nearing completion, the implementing of Wheeler's plan was essential to the continuation of the corps's mapping program and natural resources investigations. Though Wheeler had done well in the sciences and in math when he was at the U.S. Military Academy, he produced little of value to a government accustomed to the survey work of the topographical corps, the Interior Department, and the Smithsonian Institution.

Wheeler did not escape censure for disparaging Hayden's qualifications as a scientist when Wheeler appeared before the committee on Public Lands in 1874. Hayden, a geologist with an M.D. from Albany Medical College, began his career in the West in 1853 when he went on a fossil-collecting trip up the Missouri River. During the next two years he explored the region of the Missouri as far as Fort Benton, and the Yellowstone from its mouth to the confluence of the Big Horn. In 1856 and 1857 he served as surgeon and naturalist with Lt. G. K. Warren in Yellowstone, the region of the Powder River, the Loup Fork region of the Niobrara River, and the Black Hills. In 1859 and 1860 he served with Capt. William F. Raynolds in the Wind River and Absaroka Mountains.

At the onset of the Civil War, when Hayden joined the Army Medical Corps, he was better known as a paleontologist than a doctor of medicine. In 1865 he resigned his commission to become adjunct professor of geology and mineralogy at the University of Pennsylvania and then headed for the Dakota Badlands to look for more fossils.[10]

Mineral lands and the newly opened and opening farm lands under the Interior Department's jurisdiction required the expertise of geologists. After the Deficiency Appropriations bill was passed in March 1867, the unexpended monies previously used to defray the expenses of Nebraska Territory's legislative assembly became available for a geologic survey of the natural resources of the newly formed state. Hayden, with assistance from friends and colleagues, obtained the appointment to lead it.[11]

Hayden did a commendable job in Nebraska and wrote a geological report that was so well received that money was appropriated to extend his geologic survey to the Rocky Mountains. In 1869 he was appointed United States Geologist and given $10,000 to do a preliminary survey along the Front Range from Cheyenne, Wyoming, to New Mexico, via Raton Pass and Santa Fe, returning by way of Taos, the San Luis Valley and Colorado's South Park.[12]

Hayden's report on that preliminary survey was published in an edition of 8,000. It was popular, and it served him well in Congress each successive year when he needed another appropriation. In 1870, with $25,000, he returned to Wyoming to make more surveys; then he moved into northeastern Utah. Upon his return, he wrote in the preface of his 500-page report: "Never has my faith in the grand future that awaits the entire West been so strong. . . . It is my earnest desire to devote the remainder of the working days of my life to the development of its scientific and material interests, until I shall see every Territory . . . a State in the Union."[13]

As U.S. Geologist, Hayden viewed consolidation of the surveys as his opportunity to become the first director of the new Geological Survey. But Powell had other ideas as to who should direct it. Lacking membership in the National Academy, Hayden did not have its support or the clout that Powell and King had. King was appointed the new director, after which he asked Hayden to serve as one of his five principal geologists. Hayden's first assignment was a one-volume summary of the region west of the ninety-fourth meridian and north of New Mexico. After its completion Hayden worked on other projects, mostly of his own choosing, until ill health forced him to resign in 1886.[14]

Powell continues to be the best known of the western survey scientists. What fame he achieved with his Colorado River voyages was kept current with charm, administrative ability, dedication to the science of water in arid regions, and the monograph through which his ideas found permanent acceptance. His *Lands of the Arid Region of the United States,* with chapters by G. K. Gilbert, Capt. C. E. Dutton, and A. H. Thompson, continues to be the classic work of its kind.

Wheeler might have produced publications of lasting value had he conducted his surveys with more consideration for the requirements of his scientists. Forgotten are his reports on geology and mineralogy, astronomy and barometric hypsometry, paleontology, zoology, botany, archaeology, and so on. Most of his principal scientists and officers were highly qualified and capable of doing excellent work.

Lt. Rogers Birnie, who graduated first in his class at West Point in 1872, joined Wheeler in 1874. The following year he spent the better part of July and August with a small party in Death Valley, mapping and studying in detail what had been neglected in 1871. His report greatly impressed P. A. Chalfant of the *Inyo Independent* and Chalfant's son William. The report was of such historical value that William Chalfant found it indispensable in his own writings on Inyo County and Death Valley.[15] (Birnie also should be remembered for the excellence of his topographic work under exceedingly difficult conditions.)

Both Wheeler and Powell had seen the need to irrigate arid lands if they were to become useful to new settlers. There is some argument as to which one first reached that conclusion. Credit is due both of them, and also to Lt. Eric Bergland for his investigation in 1875 of "the feasibility of the diversion of the Colorado River of the West from its present channel, for the purposes of irrigation."[16] Bergland, like Bernie, also had graduated first in his class. His report on the potential of the Colorado River to irrigate the Imperial Valley in southeastern California should have been one of the more pertinent sources of information to Imperial Valley irrigators and the government when the former were pressing for government assistance in controlling the Colorado. Here, again, was a report of value, of which entrepreneurs interested in irrigation later in the nineteenth century and the congressmen they beseiged seemed unaware.

As for Wheeler's maps, Richard Bartlett in *Great Surveys of the American West* thought there had been sufficient improvement to justify continuation of Wheeler's survey until his maps were completed and remarked that the Geological Survey had not yet completed a set of topographical maps such as Wheeler was making. By then the survey not only had done topographical maps to several scales but had completed a set of geologic maps. Lists of all maps published prior to the publication of Bartlett's book in 1962 are in *Publications of the Geological Survey (1879–1961)*. Bartlett was concerned that Congress, by terminating Wheeler's survey, had been wasteful of federal funds; William Goetzmann was not. Goetzmann was concerned with the loss to the public if the latest scientific mapping techniques were not used.[17]

Another matter that deserves consideration is the role of the contour map, the base of which is the topographical map. It adds considerably to the expense of a topographical map, but without it an irrigation system such as the development of arid lands requires, could not be properly designed. Wheeler made at least one contour map and undoubtedly realized its utility but, perhaps for budgetary reasons, produced no more. Civilian-led surveys took the lead not only in the production of contour maps but in perfecting mensuration techniques to improve mapmaking in general. Clarence King and James Gardner had been experimenting with various techniques since their years together in the California Geological Survey. With completion of King's survey of the fortieth parallel, Gardner was hired by Hayden, who in 1877 published an atlas of Colorado, a marvel of mapmaking that has been much admired ever since.[18]

The defects in Wheeler's maps that caused him embarrassment before the Committee on Public Lands in 1874 suggest that his leadership may not have inspired the same perfection that the civilian leaders achieved. Powell, Hayden, and King worked right along with their geographers and topographers. Gardner, in letters home after he joined Hayden, told how they lugged hundreds of pounds of mapping instruments to gain satisfactory vantage points on the highest peaks. Mules could carry equipment only so far; the rest of the labor was on foot. On a particular trying day in August 1873, said Gardner, they worked on a 13,000-foot peak hours longer than they had expected to—their food long gone—in order to get reliable data. "Dr. Hayden worked like a hero," he said.

Wheeler's Colorado party mapped the same area but did not make it to the peak "on account of difficulties," said Gardner. Hayden's personality may have been no more pleasing than Wheeler's, but judging from Gardner's description, Hayden had a capacity for making friends: "Dr. Hayden seems to make friends everywhere and I do not wonder, for he is full of good feeling when his belligerent power is not aroused."[19]

At the hearings of the Committee on Public Lands in 1874, Powell had praised Wheeler's ability do good astronomical work, stating that it ranked with the best that had "ever been done in this country, and, perhaps, with the best" that had been done "in the world." It was Wheeler's use of outdated odometer mensuration that was spoiling his maps, and Powell had just pointed that out to the committee. "What I have stated," said Powell, "might do Lieutenant Wheeler injustice unless I state further that it is probable that he would not claim that this map was intended to represent accurately the topography of the country. He would probably claim that it was made from a meandering survey, and that it was only intended to represent the country adjacent to the line of travel." Wheeler had "marched around and looked into, but did not enter" large areas the size of Connecticut and Rhode Island together and shown those areas in preliminary maps as surveyed.[20]

Wheeler was interested in irrigation of arid lands—particularly those adjacent to mining developments—but did not see the need for detailed maps in siting irrigation systems. Powell looked at the arid West from a different perspective. He saw the need to show on maps the areas suitable for irrigated agriculture and those that were not. Entrepreneurs such as Sen. William Morris Stewart saw no limitations to developing the West and wanted no delays in opening the public lands to settlement.[21]

By the mid-1870s Wheeler had one of his parties engaged in making stream-flow measurements with a view to providing data for irrigation systems, but his efforts seemed to have had little support. By 1888 land speculators and land-hungry farmers were demanding that the public lands be opened to settlement whether or not they were arid and required irrigation systems. A bill, prepared by Senator Stewart was passed, and the Geological Survey assigned to its implementation.[22]

Powell promptly developed a program to collect the requisite stream-flow data and select sites for water impoundments. By 1890 his survey teams had identified "about 150 reservoir sites and approximately 30 million acres of irrigable land." In progress were the maps Powell felt were essential to the construction of successful irrigation systems. Stewart, in no mood for delays, soon had in motion enough congressional support to cut the Geological Survey's funding to the bone.[23] By 1894 Powell found it prudent to retire.

Wheeler, meanwhile, had been doing business with the private sector as a consultant. In 1892, ten years before the federal program to irrigate the West began, he published a pamphlet to assist private sector entrepreneurs in selecting areas where soils were suitable for irrigation.[24] Like Powell he was concerned with the potential for the success of a project, few projects having good survival records at that time. Except for overstating the opportunities for successful projects under private development, his advice was sound. Had he still been with the corps in the 1890s, the time would have been right for a second career, for Congress was then looking to the corps for expertise in developing water impoundments in the West.[25]

TEN

A Parting of the Ways

WHEELER EMPLOYED HIGHLY qualified officers and scientists. When his officers left his survey, they often rose rapidly in the ranks of the military. When his scientists left, many of them attained their goals in scientific institutions and organizations or in the Geological Survey. G. K. Gilbert found his niche with Powell after leaving Wheeler. Following consolidation of the western surveys, Gilbert continued his career in the Geological Survey, becoming chief geologist in 1889. Henry W. Henshaw, later to join the Smithsonian's Bureau of Ethnology, was employed as ornithologist and collector of natural history from 1872 to 1879. His contributions to Wheeler's annual reports from 1875 to 1879 were based on studies made in Arizona, California, Nevada, and Oregon.[1]

Wheeler had several officers with a scientific bent. One was Lt. Samuel Escue Tillman, who joined Wheeler in 1873 to take charge of a field party working in Arizona and New Mexico. Tillman used the opportunity for on-site study of geology and mineralogy. In 1876 he returned to Wheeler's employ and remained with him until 1879, serving as executive officer of parties assigned to various other western states.

Tillman's goal was to improve all aspects of education at the Military Academy.[2] Among his contributions were three textbooks, two of which include what he learned from field experience: *Elementary Mineralogy* and *Important Minerals and Rocks*. Without periods of on-site study, he could not have significantly enlarged upon what little was known about western geology and mineralogy at that time.

An officer who achieved distinction in another field was Lt. William Louis Marshall, who was with Wheeler from 1872 to 1875. We do not know what thoughts about water and power development passed through his mind while leading topographical parties along and across western rivers, but they may well have accounted in part for such inventions of his as automatic movable dams, lock gates, and valves for the management of rivers and the generation of power.[3]

Wheeler's officers Marshall, Tillman, Lyle, Hoxie, and Bernie and his scientists Gilbert, Henshaw, and others were elected to membership in the science-oriented Cosmos Club for their achievements in the earth sciences. (The prestigious club had been Powell's idea, founded at his home in 1878. Gilbert, Henshaw, and Tillman had the distinction of being accepted as founding members.)[4]

It would be a mistake to assume that Wheeler's survey was a complete waste of taxpayer's money. That it was more expensive to operate and less productive than the other surveys as of 1874 was shown by the House Committee on Public Lands. Thereafter, Wheeler gave more space in his annual reports to the reporting of his scientists and more attention to the making of topographical maps. Controversy regarding the latter continues: Did the government waste the taxpayer's money by turning his mapping program over to the Geological Survey in 1879? The question has not been answered by an expert in that field. Thomas Manning's *Government in Science* states that the Geological Survey found about 100,000 square miles (or one-third) of his maps acceptable,[5] an area nearly the size of Nevada.

It seems unlikely that Wheeler could have completed his mapping program, given the state of his health. Whether he was physically ill or mentally ill during the latter years his survey was in operation, hàs not been ascertained. Consolidation of the western surveys may have exacerbated his condition, but his lack of stamina in directing his survey was evident several years before then. After his survey was terminated his diatribes on the subject of geologists and geologic mapmaking became his main means of attracting attention. Occasionally Senator Stewart, during the years 1890 to 1892 when he was bashing Powell, chided the government for terminating Wheeler's survey. However, Wheeler and Stewart no longer were closely associated, and Elliott Russell's biography of Stewart does not mention Wheeler.[6]

The absence in Wheeler's life of close ties with friends and family is apparent. Wheeler's friends Lockwood and Lyle and most of his civilian assistants and others who had become involved in Lyons and Wheeler

Mining Company during 1871 and 1872 were not likely to remain Wheeler's friends. A history of the Francis Preston Blair family, into which Wheeler married, does not mention him; in 1874, he married Lucy, granddaughter of Francis Blair. Genealogy books on the Wheelers of Massachusetts mention Wheeler only in passing.[7] Wheeler was all but forgotten when historians got around to writing about the western surveys. Then, disadvantaged by the paucity of information about him, they did what they could with an elusive and enigmatic man.

Wheeler rode roughshod over the strong as well as the weak—those with savvy as well as those who were gullible. Even the powerful could not make him change his ways. When Wheeler failed to mention Maj. Gen. W. H. Emory's mapping contributions in 1874 while expounding on his own and those of the predecessors he wished to credit, Emory fought back in the press. No records show any remorse on Wheeler's part. Alienating a superior seemed of no importance to him.[8]

In 1875 the edited version of Wheeler's 1869 reconnaissance in Nevada was published. Col. James Simpson did not get around to reading it until 1876. In it, he found that the name he had given to Union Peak, the highest peak in Nevada, had been changed to Wheeler Peak. While mapping a wagon road across Nevada in 1859, Simpson had discovered the 13,000-foot peak. In honor of Jefferson Davis, then the secretary of war, Simpson named the peak for him. When Davis joined the Confederacy, Simpson renamed it Union Peak, and as such it appeared on maps.

One can imagine Simpson's consternation when he read in Wheeler's report: "This Peak has been called indiscriminately on published maps, Union or Jeff. Davis Peak." On June 30, 1876, Simpson wrote Humphreys the details of the naming of the peak,[9] and on July 5 Humphreys referred the letter to Wheeler for appropriate action. Wheeler responded as follows on the seventh: "The name 'Wheeler Peak' will be withdrawn from the original and subsequent published maps, an action long since contemplated."[10] Wheeler did nothing of the kind and Wheeler Peak it continued to be.

By 1877 Wheeler began to feel publicly the brunt of having lost Gilbert to Powell. Gilbert's *Report on the Geology of the Henry Mountains,* which addresses volcanism, established him as a scientist of extraordinary ability. Another loss to Wheeler was James Gardner, who had approached him as well as Hayden for a position following the completion of King's survey. Wheeler may not have realized that Gardner was likely to approach Hayden as well and delayed in stating the terms of employment. In the interim Gardner was engaged by Hayden. Hayden's

Colorado Atlas, which also appeared in 1877, was a tribute to Gardner as well.

In 1878 Wheeler made Lt. Tillman chief of a party doing sextant and triangulation work, one of seven parties so engaged. So ambitious a program to obtain data for maps indicates a considerable change in priorities from the previous years. The passage of the Sundry Civil Expenses Act in June may have been the reason.[11] Consolidation of the surveys was in the air, and before the year was out the report of the National Academy was ready for congressional action.

Wheeler was not dispossessed of his job in 1879. He had annual reports to complete and volume 1 of his Final Report to write before taking on other projects for the corps. His early leaves of absence were not sick leaves. In June 1880 he took leave until October and then asked for a two-month extension. From then on he took extensive leaves, often of six months' duration.[12]

By 1883 Wheeler was thinking of retiring and reported in June for a physical examination. He was granted a leave of absence to October instead. On March 6, 1884, he was placed on sick leave, and on March 29 the *Army and Navy Journal* reported him as still "seriously ill" at his residence in Washington, D.C. In June 1888 he retired following a series of other extended six-month leaves of absence.[13]

On May 17, 1890, the *Army and Navy Journal* reported a congressional authorization had been obtained to make Captain Wheeler a major, the rank to which he would have been entitled had he not retired prematurely. On December 5, it reported: "Major George M. Wheeler and Mrs. Wheeler sailed for Liverpool Wednesday on the steamer *Majestic.*"[14]

Following retirement Wheeler divided his time between New York City and Washington, D.C. On February 3, 1902, Lucy Wheeler died in New York City. "She had long suffered from spinal disease and her death was not unexpected."[15] Wheeler's death followed on May 4, 1905. They had suffered years of illness and worry, and when Wheeler died, he was destitute. He was to be buried in a pauper's grave when an obituary in the *New York Times* was seen by a reader who got in touch with Lt. Col. Daniel Lockwood. Lockwood arranged for Wheeler's burial at West Point.[16]

APPENDIX A

"'Role'' Call

BELKNAP AND GRANT

President Ulysses S. Grant, who took office on March 4, 1869, appointed William Worth Belknap as secretary of war in October. Belknap served in that position from November 1, 1869, until he resigned in March 1876, following impeachment for malfeasance. He was a lawyer, practicing in Keokuk, Iowa, until the Civil War. During the war he served as an officer, rising to the rank of brigadier general in 1864. After his resignation, he resided first in Philadelphia and then in Washington, D.C., where he practiced law.

Grant's two terms as president extended to March 3, 1877. His position on the consolidation of the western surveys is reflected in correspondence supplied to the House Committee on Public Lands in April 1874.

BELL, WILLIAM

Bell, whose career spanned the years from 1848 to 1905, was first active as a Daguerrean in Philadelphia. In 1851 he exhibited at the Institute of American Manufactures. From 1865 to 1869 he was active in Washington, D.C., as chief photographer of the Army Medical Museum.

Bell's work in the West is limited to the months he was with Wheeler, who had many of his photographs, along with those of O'Sullivan, reproduced in large editions for circulation. Bell spent the latter part of his career in Philadelphia, where he operated his own studio. He formed a photographic publishing venture with George Barrie and Sons in 1885. He was active until five years before his death in 1910, probably in Philadelphia. Little is known of Bell's early years beyond that he was born in England in 1830. (For this sketch I am indebted to Kenneth Finkel's *Nineteenth-Century Photography in Philadelphia* [New York: Dover, 1980].)

DELANO, COLUMBUS

Delano was an Ohio congressman when he was appointed by President Grant in 1869 to be commissioner of internal revenue. Subsequently made secretary of the interior by Grant, Delano served in that capacity from November 1, 1870, until fraud in the Bureau of Indian Affairs brought his political career to a close in October 1875. He retired to Mount Vernon, Ohio, where he died in 1896.

FOUNTAIN, SAMUEL WARREN

Fountain was 18 when he enlisted in the Civil War. In 1866, he was appointed to the U.S. Military Academy from Ohio. He graduated in June 1870 and was assigned to New Mexico in September as a second lieutenant in the Eighth Cavalry. He was at Fort Wingate from November 1870 to June 1874. There, his considerable executive ability impressed his superior, who assigned him to the position of acting assistant quartermaster.

What motivated the court-martial proceedings against Fountain in 1874 is not clear in the hearing record on file at the National Archives. Fountain was relieved of duty at Fort Wingate and assigned to Fort McRae, New Mexico. Following the court-martial hearing in December 1875 he was assigned to Texas, where he served at various posts until October 1886. He was promoted to first lieutenant in October 1878, to captain in 1889, and to assistant adjutant general in 1891.

Fountain served in campaigns against Geronimo in 1885–86 and against the Sioux in 1890–91. He resigned from the army in April 1905, one day after he was promoted to brigadier general. *Who's Who in America* (1912–13) lists him as a member of the National Geographical Society.

GARDINER, JAMES TERRY

Like Fountain, the association of James Gardiner (or Gardner) with Wheeler's survey was peripheral. Gardiner, a close friend of Clarence King, had served with the King survey of the fortieth parallel as chief topographer. Fieldwork for that survey was completed in 1872, after which Gardiner notified Hayden and Wheeler that he would be interested in another survey appointment. Hayden appears to have immediately decided to engage Gardiner as geographer, whereas Wheeler appears to have been slow to make up his mind.

Disadvantaged by having little to show the Committee on Public Lands in the way of accurate maps and other accomplishments during the May 1874 hearing, Wheeler disparaged Gardiner as well as Hayden. In a prepared statement to the committee, Gardiner had compared adversely Wheeler's mapping practices with those of the civilian-led survey leaders. In response, Wheeler tried to impugn Gardiner's integrity, charging that Gardiner had taken a position with Hayden after accepting one from him, and that Gardiner was accepting payment from the government for finishing up work on King's survey at the same time he was taking payment for work on Hayden's survey. Gardiner stated that he had not understood there was a firm offer of employment from Wheeler, and that the work for King was free of charge.

Gardiner's letters home while with Hayden in 1873 and 1874, as well as his statements before the Public Lands Committee, are descriptive of the work he and other survey personnel engaged in at that time. Thereafter, he returned to New York, where he directed the State Geological Survey from 1876 to 1886.

Gilbert, Grove Karl

Gilbert excelled in mathematics and Greek while attending the University of Rochester and became interested in natural history and geology shortly before he graduated in 1862. Following a stint of teaching, he returned to the university to work with H. A. Ward, a recognized leader in the field of natural science. In 1869 Gilbert went to Ohio to work as a volunteer in the state Geological Survey with J. S. Newberry, then professor of geology at Columbia University. In 1871 Newberry recommended Gilbert to Wheeler, who engaged him as chief geologist. Gilbert resigned in 1874.

During the years Gilbert worked for John Wesley Powell, he became widely known for his published monographs and for his lectures at Cornell, Columbia, and Johns Hopkins. The latter years of his career were spent in Berkeley as a guest of the University of California. There he did the experiments that enabled him to write *The Transportation of Debris by Running Water,* published by the Geological Survey in 1914.

Hoxie, Richard L.

Lieutenant Hoxie, one of Wheeler's executive officers from 1872 to 1874, was educated in New York, Pennsylvania, Italy, and Iowa, where he attended Iowa State University in 1861. In 1868 he graduated from the U.S. Military Academy. After leaving the Wheeler survey in 1874, he was active mainly in Washington, D.C. His wife, Vinnie Ream Hoxie, a sculptor, became one of the city's most popular hostesses. Hoxie retired from the military in 1908 as a brigadier general.

Humphreys, Andrew Atkinson

Humphreys was a civil engineer with the U.S. Topographical Engineers before that branch of the military was merged with the Army

Corps of Engineers during the Civil War. In 1854 he had charge of the explorations and surveys ordered by Congress "to ascertain the most practicable and economical route for a railway from the Mississippi River to the Pacific Ocean."

With the rank of brigadier general, Humphreys served as chief of the Corps of Engineers from 1866 to 1879, when he retired from the corps and resigned from the National Academy of Sciences. His last years with the corps were marred by the controversy over which department of the government should have jurisdiction over the mapping of public lands. His resignation from the academy was occasioned by the stand it took and the pressure it exerted on Congress to consolidate the western surveys and bring them under civilian control.

LOCKWOOD, DANIEL WRIGHT

Lieutenant Lockwood graduated from the U.S. Military Academy with Wheeler in 1866. Like Wheeler he worked briefly in San Francisco for Gen. E. O. C. Ord. After returning to the corps, he served as one of Wheeler's executive officers in 1871. Thereafter, his assignments were principally related to harbor and inland waterway improvements. He retired in September 1909 with the rank of colonel.

LORING, FREDERICK WADSWORTH

Loring attended Phillips Academy in Andover, Massachusetts, before entering Harvard University in 1866. Following graduation in 1870, he worked briefly as assistant editor of the Boston *Saturday Evening Gazette* and wrote short stories, poems, and a play called *Wild Rose*.

When Wheeler's boat party disembarked at Diamond Creek in the Grand Canyon, Loring accompanied a party to Fort Whipple near Prescott, arriving early in November 1871. From there he boarded a stage for San Francisco with civilian assistants Peter Hamel and George Salmon. Near Wickenburg, Arizona, they were killed by Indians when the stage was robbed. Loring had shared Wheeler's antipathy for Indians. Furthermore, Wheeler had expected Loring to play a key role in publicizing the work of the survey.

LYLE, DAVID ALEXANDER

Lyle, a graduate of the U.S. Military Academy in 1865, was a second lieutenant in the Second U.S. Artillery in Alaska when he was transferred to Wheeler's 1871 survey. From 1872 to 1875, he was an assistant professor of philosophy at the academy. Thereafter assigned to special duty with the Coast Guard, he distinguished himself by inventing the life-saving guns, projectiles, and apparatus that bear his name. He later obtained a bachelor's degree in mining engineering at the Massachusetts Institute of Technology.

Marshall, William Louis

Marshall served in the Civil War as a private before attending the U.S. Military Academy. He graduated from the academy in 1868 and taught there during 1870 and 1871. From 1872 to 1876 he was with the Wheeler survey. Marshall Pass in Colorado, discovered in 1873 while Marshall was en route to civilization in search of a dentist, and Marshall Basin, where he discovered gold placers in the San Juan Mountains in 1875, were named for him. Described as a man of "sound judgment and bold initiative," his reputation was made in hydraulic engineering.

Ord, Edward Otho Cresap

Following graduation from the U.S. Military Academy in 1839 Ord was assigned to the Third Artillery and subsequently served in the campaign against the Seminole Indians in the Florida Everglades. He was assigned to the Department of California in 1847 for a decade or so, during which he campaigned against the Rogue River Indians of Oregon in 1856 and then the Spokane Indians in Washington Territory. In 1861 he was appointed brigadier general of volunteers for active duty in the Civil War. From 1868 to 1871 he headed the Department of California, where his duties included the coastal states and territories, Nevada, and Arizona. He was next assigned the Department of the Platte, followed by the Department of Texas, where he remained until 1880, retiring in December.

O'Sullivan, Timothy H.

O'Sullivan was a baby when his parents left Ireland for the United States and settled on Staten Island. The family's proximity to New York City enabled him to work for Mathew Brady at an early age. When Brady opened a studio in Washington, D.C., O'Sullivan also worked for him there. In 1863 O'Sullivan left Brady to work for Alexander Gardner. Gardner's practice of crediting the employee who took the photograph brought O'Sullivan's name before the public.

The excellence of O'Sullivan's work attracted the attention of Clarence King in 1867 and Wheeler in 1870. Although the 1870 survey did not materialize, Wheeler got O'Sullivan for 1871 and again from 1873 until O'Sullivan left for other employment. That O'Sullivan was given no more fieldwork after 1874 is regrettable and not only because his western work came to a close. Years of darkroom processing of photographs without respite may have hastened his death, given the toxicity of the chemicals he used. Ill with tuberculosis, he returned to the family home on Staten Island, just five months after he was hired by the Treasury Department. He was 42 when he died on January 14, 1882.

The paucity of reliable information on O'Sullivan makes him a poor subject for biographical treatment, leaving writers to engage in speculation. For example, some have incorrectly credited him with having written, under a pseudonym, "Photographs from the High Rockies," published in 1869 in *Harper's New Monthly Magazine*. O'Sullivan was not close to Wheeler and King as some say. His antics amused them, and his willingness to undertake all manner of duties brought him a closer association with them than otherwise would have been possible, but he was not viewed as a social equal. It is the importance of his photography that has made him a celebrity in the fields of art and history.

SCHOFIELD, JOHN MCALLISTER

After graduating from the U.S. Military Academy in 1853, Schofield obtained a law degree from the University of Chicago. Before serving in the Civil War, he taught natural philosophy for five years at the Military Academy and physics for one year at the University of Washington. He served briefly as secretary of war before his assignment to the Division of the Pacific in 1870.

STEWART, WILLIAM MORRIS

Stewart began his law career in California in 1850 and continued it in Nevada in 1860. There he became known for his ability to develop mining laws that benefited the mining industry. He was a U.S. senator from 1864 to 1875 and from 1887 to 1905, intermittently practicing law in California as well as Nevada.

VAN VLIET, STEWART

Van Vliet, a graduate of the U.S. Military Academy in 1840, attained the rank of colonel in June 1872. He served as quartermaster of the Department of the Missouri from October 1874 to July 1875.

WYANT, ALEXANDER HELWIG

Wyant grew up on an Ohio farm and was 21 before he saw an art exhibition. He was not yet 30 when his landscape work began attracting attention in New York City. In 1868 he was elected an associate member of the National Academy of Design and a full member the following year. From 1866 to 1873, the year Wheeler engaged him, his paintings had been shown thirty-two times in major eastern cities. His understanding of nature and the dexterity he achieved with his left hand enabled him to do even more important paintings after his unfortunate experience at Fort Wingate than he had before. His reputation as one of America's greatest landscape artists remains secure.

APPENDIX B

Wheeler's Selection of O'Sullivan and Bell Photographs

The following list of photographs was copied from a pamphlet in the Wheeler files at the National Archives. There are many others, some without captions. The views included in the list of sets that concludes Appendix B may or may not correspond entirely with the list of views in the pamphlet.

List of Landscape and Stereoscopic Views taken in connection with Geographical Explorations and Surveys West of the One Hundredth Meridian

LANDSCAPE VIEWS

1871 [O'SULLIVAN]

1. Snow Peaks, Bull Run Mining District, Nevada.
2. Group of Pah-Ute Indians, Nevada.
3. Bluff opposite Big Horn Camp, Black Cañon, Colorado River.
4. Black Cañon, Colorado River, looking below, from Big Horn Camp.
5. Black Cañon, Colorado River, looking above, from Camp 7.
6. Black Cañon, Colorado River, looking below, near Camp 7.
7. Black Cañon, Colorado River, looking below, near Camp 7.
8. Black Cañon, from Camp 8, looking above.
9. Black Cañon, Colorado River, looking above, from Mirror Bar.
10. Entrance to Black Cañon, Colorado River, from above.
11. Wall in the Grand Cañon, Colorado River.

12. Cereus Giganteus, Arizona.
13. Water Rhyolites, near Logan Springs, Nevada.
14. Rock carved by drifting sand, below Fortification Rock, Ariz.
15. Iceberg Cañon, Colorado River, looking above.
16. Alpine Lake, in the Sierra Nevada, California.

1872 [Bell]

1. Cañon of Kanab Wash, Colorado River, looking south.
2. Cañon of Kanab Wash, Colorado River, looking north.
3. Cañon of Kanab Wash, Colorado River, looking south.
4. Cañon of Kanab Wash, Colorado River, looking south.
5. Colorado River, mouth of Kanab Wash, looking west.
6. Grand Cañon, Colorado River, near Paria Creek, looking west.
7. Grand Cañon, Colorado River, near Paria Creek, looking west.
8. Grand Cañon, Colorado River, near Paria Creek, looking east.
9. Looking south into the Grand Cañon, Colorado River.
10. Rain Sculpture, Salt Creek Cañon, Utah.
11. Grand Cañon of the Colorado River, mouth of Kanab Wash, looking west.
12. Grand Cañon of the Colorado River, mouth of Kanab Wash, looking east.
13. Grand Cañon of the Colorado River, mouth of Kanab Wash, looking west.
14. Perched Rock, Rocker Creek, Arizona.
15. Limestone Walls, Kanab Wash, Colorado River.

1873 [O'Sullivan]

1. Apache Lake, Sierra Blanca Range, Arizona.
2. View of Apache Lake, Sierra Blanca Range, Arizona.
3. View of Apache Lake, Sierra Blanca Range, Arizona. (Two Apache scouts in foreground.)
4. North Fork Cañon, Sierra Blanca Creek, Arizona.
5. Cooley's Park, Sierra Blanca Range, Arizona.
6. Distant View of Camp Apache, Arizona.
7. Aboriginal life among the Navajo Indians, near old Fort Defiance, New Mexico [*sic:* Arizona Territory].
8. Historic Spanish record of the conquest, south side of Inscription Rock, New Mexico.
9. Historic Spanish record of the conquest, south side of Inscription Rock, New Mexico. (No. 3.)
10. Ancient ruins in the Cañon de Chelle, New Mexico [*sic:* Arizona Territory], in a niche fifty feet above the present canon-bed.

11. The Church of San Miguel: the oldest in Santa Fe, N. Mex.
12. Looking across the Colorado River, to mouth of Paria Creek.
13. Cañon of the Colorado River, near mouth of San Juan River, Arizona [*sic:* Utah.].
14. South side of Inscription Rock, New Mexico.
15. Cañon de Chelle, New Mexico [*sic:* Arizona Territory]. Walls of the Grand [*sic*] Cañon about 1,200 feet in height.
16. Head of Cañon de Chelle, New Mexico [*sic*], looking down. Walls about 1,200 feet in height.
17. Indian Pueblo, Zuni, N. Mex.; view from the south.
18. Old Mission Church, Zuni Pueblo, N. Mex.; view from the plaza.
19. Section of south side of Zuni Pueblo, N. Mex.

STEREOSCOPIC VIEWS

1871 [O'SULLIVAN]

1. The start from Camp Mojave, Arizona, September 15, 1871.
2. Nee-chi-qua-ra, a good specimen of the Mojave type.
3. Camp in Painted Cañon, Colorado River.
4. First halt within the Black Cañon. Walls 1,500 feet.
5. Snug Harbor, Black Cañon; halt for the night.
6. Light and Shadow, Black Cañon. Walls about 1,700 feet in height.
7. Middle of Black Cañon, looking downstream. Walls from 800 to 1,200 feet.
8. View from Black Cañon; the grand walls in perspective.
9. View down Black Cañon from Mirror Bar; the walls repeated by reflection.
10. Mojave Indians caught napping.
11. Melon-cactus (*Cereus ctenoides*), three feet in height and sixteen inches in diameter.
12. Camp at crossing of the Colorado, just below the mouth of the Grand Cañon.
13. Triangulation-station near the mouth of the Grand Cañon, Colorado River.
14. Grotto Spring, Grand Cañon, Colorado River.
15. View of the Grand Cañon of the Colorado. Characteristic walls, 5,000 feet high.
16. Maiman, a Mojave Indian, guide and interpreter.
17. Baptismal Font, about six miles above the mouth of the Grand Cañon.
18. View across the Grand Cañon, from Grotto Spring.
19. Grand Cañon, junction of Diamond and Colorado Rivers.

20. View of Grand Cañon walls, near mouth of Diamond River.
21. Types of Mojave Indians.
22. Fred W. Loring in his campaign-costume, with his mule "Evil Merodach."
23. View across the crater of San Francisco Mountain.

1872 [Bell]

1. Mormon village of Mona, below the foothills of Nebo Peak, Wahsatch Range.
2. Small artificial lake for irrigating-purposes at Mona.
3. A gravel-bed carved by the rain, Salt Creek Cañon, Utah.
4. Sevier River Valley, to the south of Gunnison, Utah.
5. View in the high country on the headwaters of the Dirty Devil River.
6. Mountain-range near Fish Lake. Altitude, 11,575 feet.
7. View in the high country on the headwaters of the Dirty Devil River.
8. Three Lakes Cañon; gray cliffs in the distance; near Kanab, Utah.
9. Cave near Kanab, Utah.
10. Near Jacob's Pool, in Northern Arizona.
11. The "Vermilion Cliff," a typical plateau edge, as seen from Jacob's Pool, Arizona.
12. A perched block of sandstone, being gradually undermined by action of sand and wind.
13. "The Bear," a mass of sand-stone fallen from the cliffs.
14. The cañon of Kanab Creek, near its junction with the Grand Cañon of the Colorado.
15. "The Bath," a dripping spring in Kanab Cañon.
16. The cañon of Kanab Creek, near its junction with Grand Cañon of the Colorado.
17. The cañon of Kanab Creek, near its junction with Grand Cañon of the Colorado.
18. The cañon of Kanab Creek, near its junction with Grand Cañon of the Colorado.
19. The cañon of Kanab Creek, near its junction with Grand Cañon of the Colorado.
20. The cañon of Kanab Creek, near its junction with Grand Cañon of the Colorado.
21. The cañon of Kanab Creek, near its junction with Grand Cañon of the Colorado.
22. The mouth of Kanab Creek.
23. Sand sculpture.
24. Grand Cañon, mouth of Kanab Wash. Walls, 1,800 feet in height.
25. The Grand Cañon of the Colorado, near the mouth of Kanab Creek.
26. Yellow pine (*Pinus ponderosa,* Doug.).

27. Colorado River, above the mouth of the Paria. Walls, 2,100 feet in height.
28. Marble Cañon, one of the gorges of the Colorado, here 1,200 feet deep.
29. Marble Cañon, one of the gorges of the Colorado, here 1,200 feet deep.
30. Marble Cañon, one of the gorges of the Colorado, here 1,200 feet deep.
31. Devil's Anvil, near foot of To-ro-weap Valley. River 3,000 feet below.
32. The northern wall of the Grand Cañon of the Colorado.
33. The northern wall of the Grand Cañon of the Colorado.
34. The Grand Cañon of the Colorado, near the foot of To-ro-weap Valley.
35. The Grand Cañon of the Colorado, near the foot of To-ro-weap Valley.
36. The Grand Cañon of the Colorado, near the foot of To-ro-weap Valley.
37. The Grand Cañon of the Colorado, near the foot of To-ro-weap Valley.
38. The Grand Cañon of the Colorado, near the foot of To-ro-weap Valley.
39. Grand Cañon, foot of To-ro-weap Valley.

1873 [O'SULLIVAN]

1. Zuni Indian girl, with water olla.
2. Alcalde, or municipal officer of the Zuni Indians.
3. The two "beauties"; Zuni Indian belles, sixteen and eighteen years of age.
4. Lieutenant-governor of the Zuni Indians.
5. Gardens surrounding the Indian pueblo of Zuni.
6. Group of Zuni Indian "braves" at their pueblo, New Mexico.
7. Group of Zuni Indians at their pueblo, or town, New Mexico.
8. War-chief of the Zuni Indians.
9. Old Mission Church, pueblo of Zuni.
10. Old Spanish record on north wall of Inscription Rock, N. Mex.
11. Distant view of ancient ruins, Cañon de Chelle, New Mexico [*sic:* Arizona Territory].
12. Ruins in Cañon de Chelle, New Mexico [*sic*].
13. View looking down the Cañon de Chelle, about fifteen miles below the head.
14. Circle Wall, Cañon de Chelle.
15. Explorer's Column, Cañon de Chelle, New Mexico [*sic*].

16. Central portion of Cañon de Chelle, New Mexico [*sic*].
17. Camp Beauty, Cañon de Chelle. Walls, 1,200 feet high.
18. View near head of Cañon de Chelle, New Mexico [*sic*].
19. Cañon de Chelle.
20. Aboriginal life among the Navajo Indians, Cañon de Chelle, New Mexico [*sic*].
21. Navajo Indian squaw and child.
22. Navajo squaws and child, Cañon de Chelle, New Mexico [*sic*] .
23. Navajo boys and squaw in front of the quarters at old Fort Defiance, New Mexico [*sic*].
24. Navajo brave and his mother.
25. Domestic scene among the Navajos.
26. Navajo Indian dance.
27. Apache Lake, summit of Sierra Blanca Mountains, Arizona.
28. Cooley's Ranch, ten miles east of Camp Apache, Arizona.
29. Coyotero Apache scouts, at Apache Lake, Sierra Blanca Range, Arizona.
30. Apache Indians as they appear ready for the war-path.
31. Apache squaw and papoose.
32. Apache braves, ready for the trail, Arizona.
33. Young Apache warrior and his squaw, near Camp Apache, Ariz.
34. Pedro, captain of one of the Coyotero Apache bands, Arizona.
35. Apache squaw and child.
36. Cañon of the Colorado River, Utah, twenty-five miles above the mouth of Paria Creek.*
37. The ancient Church of San Miguel, Santa Fe, N. Mex.
38. Altar, Church of San Miguel, Santa Fe, N. Mex.

Landscape Views

Bound Sets—50 each

12 for the Secretary of War
12 for the Chief of Engineers
16 for the Lieutenant Wheeler

Bound Sets—25 each

60 for the Secretary of War

10 Sets 50 each unbound Chief of Engrs. office

80 Sets 25 each unbound for the Secretary of War
80 Sets 25 each unbound for the Chief of Engineers
80 Sets 25 each unbound for Lieutenant Wheeler

Stereoscopic Views

17 Sets	)		Secretary of War
17 Sets	)	100 each	Chief of Engineers
16 Sets	)		Lieutenant Wheeler
100 Sets	)		Secretary of War
100 Sets	)	50 each	Secretary of War
100 Sets	)		Lieutenant Wheeler

[Dated] January 23/75

*This and other captions of O'Sullivan's photographs of the Colorado River taken twenty-five miles or more above Paria Creek cannot be authenticated with repeat photography. Apparently no attempt was made to do so prior to constructing Glen Canyon Dam, and the filling of Lake Powell precludes doing so now. We can only speculate about what O'Sullivan did during the week or so he was at Lee's Ferry beyond taking some photographs of the immediate area; intent on pleasing Wheeler, he may well have fabricated No. 36 and possibly others. One caption on a photograph at the Library of Congress would have us believe he was near the Crossing of the Fathers; another, that he was near the mouth of the San Juan River.

APPENDIX C

Wheeler and Congressman Logan Roots

Logan Holt Roots was born in Perry County, Illinois. He was active in various responsible positions in the army during the Civil War. In Arkansas he engaged in planting and trading. Upon readmission of Arkansas to the Union, he was elected to Congress, serving from June 22, 1868, to March 3, 1871. Wheeler's letter soliciting Roots's support for the 1871 survey follows:

San Francisco Cal
Jany 23rd 1871

My dear Sir

Your very kind favor of 16th ult has been at my hand for some time[;] meanwhile I have been very anxiously waiting for news from Washington informing me of action in progress looking to a special appropriation for the continuation of more comprehensive explorations under my charge, thru part of Nevada, Cal. & Arizona.—

You know that the trip organized for 1870 has been delayed because Gen Schofield thought it inadvisable to take so much money out of the Q.M.D. and indeed there was no surplus for the purpose—however a strong document has gone on[,] warmly recommended and approved by both Gen[erals] Ord & Schofield[,] requesting the Sec'y of War to ask Congress for a special appropriation of Fifty Thousand Dollars to run my parties up to the end of the fiscal year June 30th 1872; an official recommendation also asked that I might be ordered to W-n to make such preliminary arrangements as might be necessary, meaning in reality that

I should get there & by meeting personally the members of the various committees under whose especial eye come the interests of the Pacific Coast in the way of the development of mines & such other resources as may be benefitted [and] induce them to take favorable action as speedily as possible so that my parties could leave the RR by Apr 1st 1871.—It is not yet time to hear from this matter neither from private letters and by the above named gentlemen & myself to the Chief of Engineers. I am afraid however that if they see fit to order me to Washington that it will be too late to accomplish the result so as to take advantage of the season at the opening of Spring. I would like therefore to have you advise with me as to any further course that may be taken looking to an order temporarily or otherwise requiring me to report to the Headquarters of my Corps, for I feel certain that my presence there will be necessary in order that I may put myself in shape to have the means to promulgate[?] the exploration on the scale that I would like—

I know that the members of the Pacific Delegation all are very much in favor of a continuation of the work already begun and besides the pride that I naturally feel in carrying out a project once formed there is also a desire that my experience may be brought into use to benefit the operations of the future.—

If you will take the pains to see members of the Pacific Delegation and in referring to this matter mention your willingness to co-operate you will greatly oblige—

Very Respectfully
Your ob't serv't
/s/ Geo M Wheeler
Lieut of Engineers

Notes

Chapter 1

1. Albert Gallatin Wheeler, *The Genealogical and Encyclopedic History of the Wheeler Family in America* (Boston: American College of Genealogy, 1914), and Frederick Clifton Pierce, *History of Grafton, Worcester County, Massachusetts* (Worcester: Press of Charles Hamilton, 1879), 345.

2. Constance Wynn Altshuler, *Chains of Command* (Tucson: Arizona Historical Society, 1981), 146.

3. Annual Report of E. O. C. Ord, September 1869, *Report of the Secretary of War,* 41st Cong., 2d sess., H. Doc. 1, pt. 2 (Serial 1412).

4. George W. Cullum, *Biographical Register of the Officers and Graduates of the U.S. Military Academy at West Point* (Boston and New York: Houghton Mifflin and Company, 1891). Like Wheeler, Lieutenant Lockwood graduated from the Military Academy in June 1866. From June 4, 1869, to January 24, 1870, he served on General Ord's staff on loan from the Corps of Engineers.

5. Special Orders No. 94, Headquarters Department of California, San Francisco, June 7, 1869, reprinted on p. 1 of George M. Wheeler, *Preliminary Report of the General Features of the Military Reconnaisance* [sic] *through Southern Nevada . . . , 1869* (San Francisco: n.p., 1870).

6. Wheeler, *Preliminary Report of the General Features,* 8. On May 24, 1869, John Wesley Powell and his party left Green River, Wyoming, in three small boats to travel down the Green River through Lodore Canyon to the Colorado River, continuing through the Grand Canyon to the mouth of the Virgin River, where they disembarked on August 30.

7. Wheeler to Humphreys, February 10, 1870, W1794 3d Division, Record Group 77, National Archives. The rare first edition of Wheeler's 1869 report, cited in nn. 5 and 6, was found in a letter box of old documents not part of the Wheeler files. The title of the 1875 revised edition of Wheeler's 1869 report is *Preliminary Report upon a Reconnaissance through Southern and Southeastern Nevada, Made in 1869* (Washington D.C.: Government Printing Office, 1875).

8. Lucius Beebe and Charles Clegg, *San Francisco's Golden Era: A Picture of San Francisco before the Fire* (Berkeley, Cal.: Howell-North, 1960), 9, and Russell R. Elliott, *Servant of Power: A Political Biography of Senator William M. Stewart* (Reno: University of Nevada Press, 1983).

9. Edward O. C. Ord, *The City of the Angels and the City of the Saints or a Trip to Los Angeles and San Bernardino in 1856,* ed. Neal Harlow (San Marino, Cal.: Huntington Library, 1978), Harlow's introduction; *Dictionary of American Biography* 14:48–49; Cullum, *Biographical Register;* J. Gregg Layne, "Edward

Otho Cresap Ord: Soldier and Surveyor," *Historical Society of Southern California,* 17, no. 4: 139–42; and Doris Ostrander Dawdy, *Artists of the American West,* vol. 3 (Athens: Swallow Press/Ohio University, 1987). E. O. C. Ord (1818–83), the third of twelve children, was joined in California by one sister and four brothers: Georgina, James, Robert, Pacificus, and William. Pacificus, a lawyer and rancher, was a member of the 1849 Constitutional Convention. The general was versatile, talented, and self-assured, as were most successful newcomers. Both Ord and his son Edward, Jr., were accomplished amateur painters, and it is likely that William possessed enough talent to serve as Wheeler's sketch artist. No sketches appear in the report.

10. Frank N. Schubert, *Vanguard of Expansion: Army Engineers in the Trans-Mississippi West, 1819–1879,* Historical Division, Office of Administrative Services, Office of the Chief of Engineers (Washington, D.C.: Government Printing Office, 1980; reprint, 1987), 5.

11. Rossiter W. Raymond, *Mineral Resources of the States and Territories West of the Rocky Mountains* (Washington, D.C.: Government Printing Office, 1869–77). Raymond, a graduate of Brooklyn Polytecnic School who also studied at Freiberg, Munich, and Heidelberg, was a consulting mining engineer and editor and proprietor of *American Journal of Mining* when he was appointed special commissioner. His annual reports covering 1868 to 1875 were in great demand and widely distributed.

12. Wheeler, *Preliminary Report of the General Features,* 1–17. For more information on the Mormon villages and the Muddy River, see Helen S. Carlson, *Nevada Place Names: A Geographical Dictionary* (Reno: University of Nevada Press, 1974), 174, 208, 243. The Muddy River along which the three Mormon villages were located may have derived its name from the Indian word for fertile, which sounded like "muddy" to the pioneers. Except during rain storms, the river water ran clear.

13. Ibid., 19–20.

14. Ibid.

15. Ibid; Don Ashbaugh, *Nevada's Turbulent Yesterday* (Los Angeles: Westernlore Press, 1963); Federal Writers' Project, Nevada (Portland, Ore.: Binfords & Mort, 1940); Gilman M. Ostrander, *Nevada: The Great Rotten Borough, 1859–1964* (New York: Alfred A. Knopf, 1966); and Stanley W. Paher, *Nevada Ghost Towns and Mining Camps* (Berkeley, Cal.: Howell-North, 1970).

16. Wheeler, *Preliminary Report of the General Features,* 7.

17. Ibid., 8.

18. Ibid., 10.

Chapter 2

1. Endorsement of General Humphreys regarding claim of Henry Custer for unpaid wages, 692GR1871, Record Group 77, NA; it was through this claim that the author learned of the aborted 1870 reconnaissance. George M. Wheeler to Humphreys, September 9, 1870, W2047 3d Division, Record Group 77, Na-

tional Archives, requesting permission to hire T. H. O'Sullivan for $150 per month.

2. Endorsement of General Humphreys, n. 1.

3. Asit K. Biswas, *History of Hydrology* (Amsterdam: North-Holland Publishing Company, 1970), 291, 293, 319. Humphreys also was a member of the American Philosophical Society, the American Academy of Arts and Sciences, and honorary or corresponding member of societies in Austria, France, and Italy. A doctor of laws degree was conferred on him by Harvard University. *Dictionary of American Biography* 5:371.

4. Frank N. Schubert, *Vanguard of Expansion: Army Engineers in the Trans-Mississippi West, 1819–1879,* Historical Division, Office of Administrative Services, Office of the Chief of Engineers (Washington, D.C.: Government Printing Office, 1980; reprint, 1987), 109; Robert Taft, "Illustrators of the Pacific Railroad Reports," The Kansas Historical Quarterly (November 1951); and Dictionary of American Biography.

5. Wheeler to Congressman Logan H. Roots, January 23, 1871, 209GR 1871, Record Group 77, National Archives.

6. Ibid., and Rodman W. Paul, *Mining Frontiers of the Far West, 1848–1880* (New York: Holt, Rinehart and Winston, 1963), 37–55.

7. Roots to Humphreys, February 2, 1871, 209GR1871, Record Group 77, National Archives. Roots's remarks during the second and third sessions of the 41st Congress, and the bills he sponsored, as reported in the *Congressional Globe,* do not deal with mining or exploration.

8. Humphreys to Wheeler, March 23, 1871, in *Annual Report of the Chief of Engineers,* 42d Cong., 2d sess., S. Doc. 65 (Serial 1479), 3–4; Wheeler to Humphreys, February 21, 1871, 323GR1871, Record Group 77, National Arhives; and Adjutant General's Office, Special Orders No. 109, March 18, 1871, Record Group 92, National Archives. (The obedience to official orders of John C. Fremont can be compared with that of Wheeler. Both of them had powerful supporters in Congress who wanted inside information that was not spelled out in their orders.)

9. Ibid.

10. Return of officers and hired men, May 1871, 484GR1871, Record Group 77, National Archives.

11. Doris Ostrander Dawdy, *Artists of the American West,* vol. 3 (Athens: Swallow Press/Ohio University Press, 1985; reprint 1987).

12. Wheeler to Humphreys, August 9, 1871, 159GR1871, Record Group 77, National Archives, in which Wheeler said, "The artists have been engaged in delineations and representations, where it has been deemed desirable," presumably referred to artist Richardson and photographer O'Sullivan. The letter to Humphreys predates the disaster of October 11, when Wheeler lost his notes and illustrations. On January 23, 1872 (164GR1872), Wheeler told Humphreys that sketching had been "carried on by certain members of the parties but only in an amateur way; the only results that can serve as valuable adjuncts to a report were taken among the Cañons of the Colorado River." Most of O'Sullivan's Colorado River work survived, but much of his other work was lost in transit to

Washington, D.C. Richardson did make sketches, as noted by Gilbert, but they may have been in Wheeler's possession on October 11, in which case they were lost to the river. Rough sketches were made by Gilbert for his own purposes, and others may have done likewise. It is unlikely that Richardson made any sketches after October 11, for he assisted in manning the boats. When he reached Diamond River, he and Salmon were given a sealed communication to deliver, possibly at Prescott, where they were scheduled to take a stage to San Francisco. Salmon and most of the stage passengers were killed by Indians en route. It is not known what happened to Richardson; his name was not listed as one of the passengers.

13. Special Field Orders No. 1, *Special Orders, Special Field Orders, & Circulars,* 1871–73, Office of Chief of Engineers, Record Group 77, National Archives; G. K. Gilbert, "Notes," Accessions 3372–3388, Records of the Geological Survey, Record Group 57, National Archives; and *Annual Report of the Chief of Engineers,* 25–26.

14. Clarence King, *Geological Exploration of the Fortieth Parallel Made by Order of the Secretary of War,* vol. 3 of *Mining Industry,* by James D. Hague, with geologic contributions by Clarence King (Washington, D.C.: Government Printing Office, 1870).

15. Mary C. Rabbitt, *Minerals, Lands, and Geology for the Common Defence and General Welfare,* vol. 1 (Washington, D.C.: U.S. Geological Survey, 1979), 167, quoting the *American Journal of Science,* 3d series, 1 (1871): 219.

16. Gilbert, "Notes," Accession 3372.

17. "Wheeler and His Guides—Where Is Egan?" *Inyo Independent,* November 18, 1871; Wheeler Scrapbook, P-W 32, Bancroft Library, University of California, Berkeley; and Richard A. Bartlett, *Great Surveys of the American West* (Norman: University of Oklahoma Press, 1962, 343–44). Historians writing about Wheeler found the article in what is assumed to be Wheeler's scrapbook at the University of California's Bancroft Library. Many of the newspaper clippings were cropped so closely that names of newspapers and/or dates of issuance are missing, as in this instance. In *Great Surveys of the American West,* Bartlett quoted parts of that article and another, both adverse to Wheeler, and wondered whether the allegations were products of a frontier editor's "imagination," an editor "embittered at the survey."

18. Special Field Orders No. 3, *Special Orders.* This is the only order in 1871 that delegated executive authority to a civilian.

19. Gilbert, "Notes."

20. Stanley W. Paher, *Nevada Ghost Towns and Mining Camps* (Berkeley, Cal.: Howell-North, 1970).

21. Ibid., and Gilbert, "Notes."

22. "Wheeler and His Guides," and Circular No. 1, *Special Orders.*

23. United States Army. *Revised Regulations for the Army of the United States, 1861,* by authority of the War Department. (Philadelphia: George W. Childs, 1862).

24. Don Ashbaugh, *Nevada's Turbulent Yesterday* (Los Angeles: Westernlore Press, 1963).

25. Gilbert, "Notes," Accession 3373.

26. "Wheeler and his Guides"; Willie Arthur Chalfant, *The Story of Inyo* (Bishop, Cal.: n.p., 1933), 255–58, and *Death Valley: The Facts* (Stanford, Cal.: Stanford, London, Milford, Oxford, 1930; reprint 1953), 51–53. Later it was learned that Hahn, unsuccessful in his search for water and fearing for his life if he returned to camp, had left his personal effects and saddle to make it appear that he had perished and had ridden his mule bareback to Arizona. He was later killed in that "wild territory."

27. Annual reports of Wheeler and Lyle, in *Annual Report of the Chief of Engineers.* S. Doc. 65 (Series 1479). Lyle's report begins on p. 74.

28. Gilbert, "Notes, " Accession 3374 .

29. Ibid.

30. Ibid.

31. Special Field orders No. 21 (signed by Lyle), *Special Orders.* The order was carried out just ten days after Egan's disappearance. The reports of Wheeler and Lyle, in *Annual Report of the Chief of Engineers,* pp. 9 and 82, are misleading.

32. "Wheeler and His Guides," and Frederick W. Loring, "Into the Valley of Death: Extracts from a Journal of a March through the Death Valley of California and Nevada, in 1871," *Appleton's Journal of Literature* (November 18, 1871), 574–75.

33. Loring, "Into the Valley of Death," Ibid.

34. *Inyo Independent,* "At Last the Officers of the Wheeler Expedition Rise to Explain," January 17, 1872. This source contains a letter from Lieutenant Lyle.

35. "Wheeler and His Guides."

36. Neill C. Wilson, *Silver Stampede: The Career of Death Valley's Hell-Camp, Old Panamint* (New York: Macmillan Company, 1937), 95–96. V. A. Gregg, a lawyer in Bakersfield, California, was born in 1844. He lived mainly in Inyo and Kern counties.

37. Annual Report of Wheeler, in *Annual Report of the Chief of Engineers,* and "Wheeler and His Guides."

38. Committee on Public Lands, "Geographical and Geological Surveys West of the Mississippi," 43d Cong., 1st sess. H. Report 612 (Serial 1626), 52.

39. Federal Writers' Project, *Death Valley* (Boston: Houghton Mifflin Company, 1939), and Chalfant, *The Story of Inyo.*

40. Federal Writers Project, *Death Valley.*

41. Ibid.

Chapter 3

1. Special Field Orders No. 20, August 31, 1871, *Special Orders, Special Field Orders, & Circulars,* 1871–73, Office of Engineers, Record Group 77, National Archives. Wheeler's monthly report to Humphreys, also dated August 31 (1781GR1871, Record Group 77, National Archives) gives the location of Cottonwood Springs and states that the boat party will arrive at Camp Mojave about September 5; it will leave there with "4 Boatmen, 12 soldiers and 10 or 12

Indians with three exploring boats and one barge." In closing, he said, "The health of the entire party has been good and the condition of the animals better than could be expected after the very severe desert and mountain marches of the past month." He did not mention in this letter or in previous letters that he had been exploring in Death Valley, where he had lost two guides, nor did he mention that assistant topographer Charles E. Fellerer had left the field, too ill to continue. (Fellerer died soon afterward, according to an item in the Wheeler scrapbook at Bancroft Library.) A map that is useful in identifying locations named in Gilbert's journal and Wheeler's reports and letters is in Dennis G. Casebier's *The Mojave Road* (Norco, Cal.: King's Press, 1975).

2. G. K. Gilbert, "Notes," Accession 3375, Records of the Geological Survey, Record Group 57, National Archives.

3. Ibid., and Joseph C. Ives, *Report upon the Colorado River of the West*, 36th Cong., 1st sess., 1861, H. Doc. 90. For a view of the canyon, sketched by topographer F. W. von Egloffstein while with Ives, redrawn by J. J. Young, see William H. Goetzmann, *Exploration and Empire: The Explorer and Scientist in the Winning of the American West* (New York: Knopf, 1966), 222. For brief biographies of these early topographic artists, see Doris Ostrander Dawdy, *Artists of the American West*, vol. 1 (Athens: Swallow Press/Ohio University Press, 1980).

4. Gilbert, "Notes."

5. Ibid.

6. Ibid.

7. Ibid.

8. Ibid.; George M. Wheeler, *Report upon United States Geographical Surveys West of the One Hundredth Meridian* (Washington, D.C.: Government Printing Office, 1889), 1:164–65; and Wheeler to Humphreys, October 24, 1871 (2132GR1871, Record Group 77, National Archives).

9. Gilbert, "Notes." Compare with Wheeler, *Report upon United States Geographical Surveys*, vol. 1.

10. Gilbert, "Notes," Accession 3376, Record Group 57, National Archives.

11. Ibid.

12. Ibid.

13. Ibid.

14. Ibid.

15. Ibid.

16. Ibid.

17. Ibid.

18. Richard A. Bartlett, *Great Surveys of the American West* (Norman: University of Oklahoma Press, 1962), 336.

19. Goetzmann, *Exploration and Empire*, 397 n. 5, 468.

20. Wheeler to Humphreys, October 24, 1871.

21. Wheeler, *Report upon United States Geographical Surveys*, 1:167.

22. Frank N. Schubert, *Vanguard of Expansion: Army Engineers in the Trans-Mississippi West, 1819–1879* (Washington, D.C.: Government Printing Office, 1987), 141–42.

Chapter 4

1. Special Field Orders No. 25, October 23, 1871, *Special Orders, Special Field Orders, & Circulars,* 1871–73, Office of Engineers, Record Group 77, National Archives.

2. Mohave County, Arizona Territory, *Mining Records,* Book B, pp. 183–87 (which include mining claims made in 1872 that name McGeary as discoverer of two and Kohler discoverer of one; all these claims were filed for record on April 9, 1873), and "Wheeler and His Guides—Where Is Egan?" *Inyo Independent,* November 18, 1871.

3. Mohave County, Arizona Territory, *Deeds,* Book 2. The deed from Wheeler, and the signatories to the powers of attorney to Lyons and Wheeler Mining Company is dated February 14, 1872, but not received and filed by the Mohave county recorder until June 11, pp. 334–39. An extended deed from E. Martin Smith to Lyons and Wheeler Mining Company is dated March 1, 1872, and received and filed by the county recorder on March 19, pp. 195–99. Senator Stewart, one of the signers of a power of attorney, appeared with Wheeler before a notary public in Washington, D.C., where the February 14 deed was executed. The notary's certification states that "on the Eighteenth day of March A.D. 1872, personally appeared William M. Stewart and George M. Wheeler, parties to a certain deed bearing date the Fourteenth day of February A.D. 1872 and to be recorded in the Territory of Arizona. The said William M. Stewart and George M. Wheeler being well known to me to be the parties described in said deed, and they the said William M. Stewart and George M. Wheeler acknowledged that they each signed, sealed and delivered the said deed as their act and deed, for the uses and purposes therein named and the said George M. Wheeler, as Attorney in fact for [each of thirty-one named signatories who] acknowledged to me that he [Wheeler] as Attorney in fact for the said [each name again repeated] did sign and seal and deliver the said deed for the uses and purposes therein set forth freely and voluntarily."

4. *The Hualapai Tribe of the Hualapai Reservation, Arizona,* v. *The United States of America,* Plaintiff's Exhibit F-1, Docket No. 90, Indian Claims Commission, 1:114. Philip J. Shenon and Roy P. Full did much of the pretrial research. See also their four-volume work, "An Evaluation Study of the Mineral Resources in the Lands of the Hualapai Tribe of Indians of Arizona," for this case, decided November 19, 1962, in favor of the Hualapai.

5. *San Joaquin Valley Argus,* July 12, 1873, p. 2, col. 3. Friedlander (1823–78) was born in Germany. He came to San Francisco in 1849. By 1852 he had cornered the flour market. Described as six feet seven inches tall, this 300-pound man was an imposing figure. Intent upon obtaining a subsidized supply of water to irrigate his San Joaquin Valley lands, he sought, perhaps with Wheeler's assistance, appointment of a commission to accomplish his goal. Headed by Lt. Col. B. S. Alexander of the corps, the commission consisted of one other corps officer and a member of the U.S. Coast Survey. Their report, *Irrigation of the San Joaquin, Tulare, and Sacramento Valleys, California,* came out in 1874. Friedlander's financial difficulties are covered by Albert Shumate

in *Breadbasket of the World: California's Great Wheat Growing Era: 1860–1890* (San Francisco: Book Club of California, 1984). The "insatiable . . . land grabber" who controlled "the wheat trade of California and the entire coast," as alleged in the *Argus,* died in San Francisco on July 1, 1878.

6. *Hualapai Tribe* . . . v. *USA,* "Summary of Evaluation," p. 1.

7. For a reprint of the article, dated May 16, 1866, see p. 52, pt. 2, of Dennis G. Casebier's *The Mojave Road* (Norco, Cal.: Tales of the Mojave Road Publishing Company, 1975); also see Casebier's *Camp Beale's Springs and the Hualpai Indians* (Norco, Cal.: Tales of the Mojave Road Publishing Company, 1980), pp. 205–6 n. 14. Casebier's spelling of *Hualpai* is the one used by the War Department.

8. Casebier, *Camp Beale's Springs,* p. 203 n. 65.

9. Ibid., p. 208 n. 25.

10. George M. Wheeler, *Preliminary Report of Explorations in Nevada and Arizona* (Washington, D.C.: Government/Printing Office, 1872), 49; also published in the *Annual Report of the Chief of Engineers,* 42d Cong., 2d sess., S. Doc. 65 (Serial 1479). For an assessment of Maynard District mines, see *Hualapai Tribe* . . . v. *USA,* 1:115 and 3:192D of the Shenon and Full evaluation study. In the Maynard Mining District, 390 location and relocation notices were filed prior to July 1, 1883. However only five properties had been sufficiently developed by January 4, 1883, to "justify individual evaluations." Except for McGeary's American Flag, they appear to have been discovered by prospectors who had not been in Wheeler's employ.

11. San Francisco city directories.

12. Mohave County, Arizona Territory, *Deeds.*

13. Peter L. Guth, "George Montague Wheeler: Last Army Explorer of the American West," (diss., U.S. Military Academy, 1975), p. 63. Guth attributed Wheeler's penniless condition to lawsuits and surgical operations. Official notice from the California secretary of state, May 20, 1979, in response to a query from the author. Fires in Sacramento and the San Francisco earthquake and fire of 1906 account for the destruction of official records and court files; Washington, D.C., court files for the period Wheeler was likely to have engaged in litigation seem not to have been preserved.

Chapter 5

1. Wheeler to Humphreys, undated report of operations in Nevada and Arizona in 1871, followed by request for funds for explorations in 1872, 1593GR 1871, Record Group 77, National Archives. The file number indicates the letter was written while Wheeler was in the field, probably in August 1871.

2. George M. Wheeler, "Facts regarding the Government Land and Marine Surveys of the United States," Extract from *Report on the Third International Congress* (Washington, D.C.: Government Printing Office, 1885), 485.

3. Wheeler to Humphreys, June 8, 1872, 1322GR1872, and Humphreys's

penciled note of April 18, 1872, to the secretary of war, 615GR1872, Record Group 77, National Archives.

4. Act of June 10, 1872, 17 *United States Statutes* 367.

5. Wheeler to Humphreys, July 13, 1872, 1652GR1872, Record Group 77, National Archives. Wheeler later revised his letterhead to include *geographical* but continued to omit *geological.*

6. "Lt. Col. Engn By command" of Humphreys to Wheeler, June 24, 1872, filed with 1322GR1872, Record Group 77, National Archives.

7. Wheeler to Humphreys, October 16, 1872, from Rendezvous Camp, near Salt Lake City, 2222GR1872, Record Group 77, National Archives. This and previous letters from the field excessively stress the supervision Wheeler had given his astronomical parties.

8. Wheeler to Humphreys, July 13, 1872, from Rendezvous Camp, near Salt Lake City, 1652GR1872, Record Group 77, National Archives.

9. Special Orders (1872) Nos. 40–43 and 47, Special Field Orders Nos. 2–6, and Circular 31, *Special Orders, Special Field Orders, & Circulars,* 1871–73, Office of Engineers, Record Group 77, National Archives.

10. Wheeler, *Progress Report upon Geographical and Geological Explorations and Surveys West of the One Hundredth Meridian in 1872* (Washington, D.C.: Government Printing Office, 1874), 11.

11. Ibid.

12. Ibid., 38.

13. See Ibid. for examples of Bell's work.

14. Grove Karl Gilbert, "Notes," Accession 3382, Records of the Geological Survey, Record Group 57, National Archives.

15. Ibid. Lee, who was involved in the Mountain Meadows Massacre in 1857, was a fugitive. In 1871, at Brigham Young's request, he began developing the ferry crossing on the Colorado River that facilitated travel between Utah and Arizona. Jacob Hamblin and perhaps others had previously crossed there by boat. After ferry service was established, it no longer was necessary to use the Crossing of the Fathers some forty miles upstream. Accounts of Lee's Ferry and ranch vary markedly. This author relies mainly on Gilbert's account.

16. Gilbert, "Notes," Accession 3382.

17. Wheeler, *Progress Report,* 38.

18. Wheeler to Humphreys, October 16, 1872, 2019GR1872 and June 8, 1872, 1322GR1872, Record Group 77, National Archives.

19. Gilbert, "Notes," Accession 3382.

20. Dwight L. Smith, "Hoskaninni: A Gold Mining Venture in Glen Canyon," in *Probing the American West,* edited by K. Ross Toole, and others. (Santa Fe: Museum of New Mexico Press, 1962), 125. This well-researched conference paper covers mining data gathered by, and mining efforts of, Robert B. Stanton, during the late 1800s. For Stanton's diary, see Dwight L. Smith and C. Gregory Crampton, eds. *The Colorado River Survey: Robert B. Stanton and the Denver, Colorado Canyon and Pacific Railroad* (Salt Lake City: Howe Brothers, 1987).

21. Gilbert, "Notes," Accession 3382.

22. Wheeler, *Progress Report,* 13–27.

Chapter 6

1. C. E. Dewing, "The Wheeler Survey Records: A Study in Archival Anomaly," *The American Archivist* 27 (April 1964): 219–21.

2. Ibid., 222.

3. Ibid., 223–25.

4. Wheeler to Humphreys, July 13, 1872, 1652GR1872, Record Group 77, National Archives.

5. Ibid., and the Act of June 10, 1872, *United States Statutes,* 367, directing the War Department to establish an astronomical base to assist in the making of maps.

6. Hayden to Secretary of Interior Columbus Delano, January 17, 1873, reprinted in Hayden's *Seventh Annual Report of Progress of the United States Geological Survey of the Territories* (Washington, D.C.: Government Printing Office, 1874), 1.

7. Wheeler to Humphreys, February 3, 1873, 21GR1873, Record Group 77, National Archives.

8. Wheeler to Humphreys, June 20, 1873, 1347GR1873, Record Group 77, National Archives.

9. Office of U.S. Geographical Surveys West of the 100th Meridian, 1869–1883, Entries 361–388, Record Group 77, National Archives. Entries 379, 382, and 383 include Nell's topographical data. Entry 382 contains a printed sticker with the number of square miles for the King and Wheeler surveys: area west of one hundredth meridian, 1,443,360; area of fortieth parallel survey, 81,600; Wheeler's expedition in 1869, 25,900; in 1871, 78,950; and in 1872, 50,400. Square miles covered in 1873 totaled 72,500, according to Wheeler in *Report upon United States Geographical Surveys West of the One Hundredth Meridian* (Washington, D.C. : Government Printing Office, 1889), 1:58.

10. Northern Arizona University Library, Special Collections No. 175. The journal, advertised for sale in 1976 by a New York City book dealer, was acquired by the library through the foresight of archivist John Irwin. With his permission, the journal was edited and annotated by this author and published as "The Wyant Diary: An Artist with the Wheeler Survey in Arizona, 1873," in *Arizona and the West* 22, no. 3 (1980): 255–78. William H. Mullane, who followed Irwin as archivist, supplied the following description of Wyant's journal: "The edges of the sheets are marbled, and there is an accordian-fold pocket at the beginning of the book for separates. . . . The book has probably been compressed much of its life inasmuch as the page edges are discolored only on the extreme edges." It contains eighty-five pages of text, illustrated with very small and often roughly drawn sketches in pencil. Wyant's finished sketches, except for one small oil probably done at Kit Carson, Colorado, en route to Fort Wingate, have not survived.

11. Adjutant General's Office, Third Auditor's Accounts, Wheeler Survey, Vouchers 13 and 14, September 1–November 9, 1873, totaling $138.00, dated December 1, 1873, and filed first quarter, 1874, Record Group 217, National Archives.

12. Eleanor Richardson Gage, "Alexander H. Wyant: A Pioneer of American Landscape Painting," *Arts and Decoration* 2, no. 10 (August 1912): 350. Not

until twenty years after Wyant's death (which occurred in 1892) did authors of articles and books begin to speculate about his western experience. Those authors did not know the name of the survey or that O'Sullivan was in charge. They knew only that Wyant had been with a military party. If, as some of them wrote, Wyant went west for his health (many Easterners did at that time), he seems to have soon regained it, for he showed remarkable endurance right up to the day he returned to Fort Wingate. Some sources mentioned Wyant's need for money (an artist's dilemma, even one as prominent as Wyant). The prices then paid artists who converted their western sketches to colorful and dramatic western landscapes—Congress had just appropriated $10,000 for Thomas Moran's large painting of Yellowstone—certainly was an incentive to sketch in the West.

13. William H. Goetzmann, *Exploration and Empire: The Explorer and Scientist in the Winning of the American West* (New York: Knopf, 1966), 435, quoting William Whitman Bailey.

14. Dawdy, "The Wyant Diary," 264.

15. Ibid., 265.

16. Ibid., 266.

17. Ibid., 267–68.

18. Ibid., 270.

19. Ibid., 271.

20. C. Gregory Crampton and W. L. Rusho, "A Report on the History of Lee's Ferry, Arizona," for the National Park Service, U.S. Department of the Interior (Washington, D.C., January 1965, mimeographed, 15–16.

21. Library of Congress, Prints and Photographs Division, Stereoscopic View No. 29, Lot No. 3427.

22. Ibid., View No. 30. This view is No. 36 in Wheeler's "List of Landscape and Stereoscopic Views Taken in Connection with Geographical Explorations and Surveys West of the One Hundredth Meridian, 1871–1873," published in 1874 (see Appendix B). Lake Powell is part of Glen Canyon National Recreation Area. Maps of the area, historical data, and general information can be obtained from the U.S. Department of the Interior, the National Park Service, or the Bureau of Reclamation office at Glen Canyon Dam, Page, Arizona.

23. Crampton and Rusho, "A Report on the History of Lee's Ferry," 29.

24. Dawdy, "The Wyant Diary," 271–75.

25. Ibid., 272.

26. Ibid., 272–73.

27. Ibid., 275. Loma, Colorado, since annexed to Del Norte, was more like 250 miles distant.

28. Ibid., 277. For payments made to O'Sullivan's guides, see Adjutant General's Office, Third Auditor's Accounts, Record Group 217, National Archives, Voucher No. 80, fourth quarter 1873, November 11: "For 1 Indian Guide, from Fort Wingate via Fort Defiance to Cañons Chen-le-ah and San Juan, & return to Fort Wingate, from September 17th to November 11th, 56 days at $1.00 per day." Inasmuch as the guide deserted on or about October 24 and it was Wheeler's policy to withhold pay until fieldwork was completed, it is likely that O'Sullivan pocketed the full amount.

29. Dawdy, "The Wyant Diary," 277. Commas have been supplied in Wyant's list of foods served.

30. Ibid., 278.

31. After Wyant resumed his career, he married Arabella Locke, one of his students. Her introduction to an exhibition and sale of his paintings in 1894 dwells on the pain he endured as well as his dedication to his art: "His life was spent in and for his art, simply, lovingly, with mastery over physical suffering such as only the few who knew him well could realize." (Courtesy of Archives of American Art, M. H. de Young Memorial Museum, San Francisco.)

Bruce Crane, later to become a widely known landscape painter, first met Wyant in 1876 and began studying with him in 1879 at the suggestion of landscape painter William Hart, who described Wyant as "a great painter." Crane, who was given a key to Wyant's studio and was free to enter at will, had a long association with Wyant. "How that man did love to paint," Crane wrote in a letter to writer John Van Dyke. Crane also observed that Wyant worked much too hard and that for the last six years of his life, he had to walk sideways. It is said that Wyant did not let those extremely painful years interfere with the beauty of his work. (Eliot Clark, *Alexander Wyant* [New York: n.p., 1916], 30, and John C. Van Dyke, *American Painting and Its Tradition* [New York: Charles Scribner's Sons, 1919, 53–56.) Van Dyke's remark that the West had not impressed Wyant is incorrect. En route to Trinidad, Colorado, in 1873, Wyant wrote in his journal regarding a mountain scene: "The panorama was much more beautiful than any I have yet seen in my life."

The absence of a medical record on Wyant at Fort Wingate is strange, for hospital records for the post included military and nonmilitary outpatients as well as hospitalized patients. Such an omission suggests that the circumstances of the paralysis, if they had been recorded, might have become a problem for Wheeler or the War Department. (See *Medical History of Post, Ft. Wingate,* Adjutant General's Office, Record Group 94, National Archives.)

Chapter 7

1. Endorsement of Col. Stewart Van Vliet, February 18, 1874, Consolidated Correspondence file of the Q.M. Gen., Record Group 92, National Archives.

2. Samuel W. Fountain, PP4686—Court Martial, Q.M. Gen. Consolidated file, Record Group 92, National Archives.

3. Ibid.

4. Wheeler to Humphreys, March 22, 1873, Q.M. Gen. Consolidated Correspondence, Record Group 92, National Archives.

5. Q.M. Gen. Consolidated Correspondence, Endorsement of July 30, 1873, Record Group 92, National Archives.

6. Ibid., Endorsement of August 22, 1873.

7. Ibid., Endorsement of February 5, 1874.

8. Ibid., Endorsement of February 18, 1874.

9. Ibid., Endorsement of May 26, 1874.

10. Ibid., Endorsements of November 7, 11, and 14, 1874.

11. Gen. Thomas M. Vincent to Humphreys, July 3, 1874, 1329GR1874, Record Group 77, National Archives.

12. Committee on Public Lands, "Geographical and Geological Surveys West of the Mississippi," 43d Cong., 1st sess., H. Rept. 612 (Serial 1626), 63.

13. Ibid., 69. William Smith Herndon was a representative from Texas.

14. Richard A. Bartlett, *Great Surveys of the American West* (Norman: University of Oklahoma Press, 1962), 370.

15. Committee on Public Lands, "Geographical and Geological Surveys," 43rd Cong., 1st sess., H. Rept. 612 (Serial 1626), 67, 70. Wheeler to General John G. Foster, May 25, 1874, Record Group 77, National Archives. Wheeler to Washington Townsend, the committee's chairman, June 3, 1874, Record Group 77, National Archives. Lyons and Wheeler Mining Company was dropped from the San Francisco city and business directory after 1873–74. Humphreys to Secretary of War Belknap, July 14, 1874, 1049/1328GR1874, Record Group 77, National Archives.

16. Committee on Public Lands, "Geographical and Geological Surveys West of the Mississippi," 43d Cong., 1st sess., H. Rept. 612 (Serial 1626), 17.

17. Ibid., 18.

18. General Foster to Wheeler, May 21, 1874, attached to Voucher 24, Adjutant General's Office, Third Auditor's Accounts, third quarter 1874, Record Group 217, National Archives. Wheeler to Humphreys, July 3, 1874, 1328/1331GR 1874, Record Group 77, National Archives. Humphreys to Wheeler, July 9, 1874, 1328/1331GR1874, Record Group 77, National Archives.

19. Wheeler to Humphreys, July 3, 1874.

20. Humphreys to Wheeler, July 9, 1874, and Humphreys to Belknap, July 14, 1874.

21. Wheeler to Gilbert, February 2 and 14, 1874, press copies of letters sent by Wheeler, U.S. Engineers Office, Entry 363, Record Group 77, National Archives. Gilbert resigned on June 7; Wheeler's response of same date also is in Entry 363. The report was published as volume 3, not 4, as in Wheeler's letter of February 14.

22. Wheeler to Gilbert, October 23, 1874, Letters Sent, U.S. Engineers Office, Entry 363, Record Group 77, National Archives, stating: "In looking over the m.s. of our report, I discover that there are allusions to individuals connected with other surveys that seem hardly necessary to fully explain your proposed meaning. I have found it necessary in most cases to erase these." An assumption that Humphreys was responsible for the deletions apparently came about because he did not want Gilbert to publish in *Silliman's Journal* any information in the manuscript before the report was published.

23. Bartlett, *Great Surveys,* 368–69. William H. Goetzmann, *Exploration and Empire: The Explorer and Scientist in the Winning of the American West* (New York: Knopf, 1966), 577–86. A. Hunter Dupree, *Science in the Federal Government: A History of Policies and Activities to 1940* (Cambridge: Belknap Press of Harvard University Press, 1957; reprint, Baltimore and London: Johns Hopkins University Press, 1986), covers the struggle of the National Academy of Sciences, approved by Congress in 1863, to attain its goal as a government advisory committee.

24. Maj. Gen. W. H. Emory to Wheeler, May 21, 1874, 1332GR1874, Record Group 77, National Archives.

25. Humphreys to Belknap, July 4, 1874. Wheeler to O'Sullivan, July 6, 1874, attached to Voucher 173, fourth quarter, Adjutant General's Office, Third Auditor's Account, Record Group 217, National Archives. Voucher 173 is a detailed account of O'Sullivan's travels, errands, and expenses. Photographs at the Library of Congress (Lot 3427, Prints and Photographs Division) and at the National Archives (Still Picture Branch) show where O'Sullivan worked in 1874.

Chapter 8

1. *Special Orders, Special Field Orders & Circulars,* 1871–73, Office of Engineers, Record Group 77, National Archives, Folio 88.

2. Ibid., Folio 87.

3. Adjutant General's Office, Third Auditor's Accounts, first quarter 1874, Voucher 67, Record Group 217, National Archives.

4. Doris Ostrander Dawdy, "The Wyant Diary," *Arizona and the West* 22, no. 3 (Autumn 1980): 271.

5. Evelyn B. Measeles, *Lee's Ferry: A Crossing on the Colorado* (Boulder, Col.: Pruett Publishing Company, 1981), 25.

6. George M. Wheeler, *Annual Report upon the Geographical Explorations and Surveys West of the One Hundredth Meridian* (Washington, D.C.: Government Printing Office, 1874), 12, also published in *Annual Report of the Chief of Engineers,* 43d Cong., 2d sess., H. Doc. 1, pt. 2 (Serial 1637), 488.

7. Wheeler, *Annual Report upon the Geographical Explorations* (1874), 110, and *Annual Report of the Chief of Engineers,* 586.

8. Adjutant General's Office, Third Auditor's Accounts, first quarter 1874, for Wheeler's letter of September 1, attached to Voucher 59, Record Group 217, National Archives. The letter supports the search for the San Juan River and requests photographs of certain views in and around Santa Fe and Denver.

9. Wheeler, *Annual Report upon the Geographical Explorations* (1874), 12, and *Annual Report of the Chief of Engineers,* 488.

10. Wyant to Wheeler, January 16, 1874, Register and Digests of Letters Received, U.S. Engineer Office, Record Group 77, National Archives. Wyant's letter reached the Office of Engineers on January 18, where it was paraphrased to read: "Acknowledges receipt of Lieut Wheeler's letter and states that his sketching was mostly done in the Cañon De Chelly. Wishes O'Sullivan to send him all the photographs made while with him. Failed to find his valise at Denver & wishes to ascertain where it is." If that letter Wheeler wrote to Wyant, probably in December, is ever found, we may be closer to learning the circumstances of Wyant's employment and paralysis.

11. Wheeler to Wyant, January 20, 1874, Letters Sent, U.S. Engineer Office, Record Group 77, National Archives.

12. Wyant to Wheeler, January 31, 1874, Register and Digests of Letters Received, U.S. Engineer Office, Record Group 77, National Archives. The let-

ter which was received in the Office of Engineers on February 3 gives a description of the valise.

13. Grove Karl Gilbert, "Notes," Accession 3388 (November 29), Records of the Geological Survey, Record Group 57, National Archives.

14. Doris Ostrander Dawdy, *Artists of the American West,* vols. 1 and 3 (Athens: Swallow Press/Ohio University Press, 1980, 1985); Eliot Clark, *Alexander Wyant* (New York: n.p., 1916), 11–13; Fritiof Fryxell (ed.), *Thomas Moran: Explorer in Search of Beauty* (New York: East Hampton Free Library, 1958).

15. William H. Powell, *Powell's Records of Living Officers of the United States Army* (Philadelphia: L. R. Hamersley & Co., 1890), 636–37.

16. Ibid.

17. Wheeler, "Facts regarding the Government Land and Marine Surveys of the United States," extract from *Report on the Third International Geographical Congress* (Washington, D.C.: Government Printing Office, 1885), 467.

18. Oscar Handlin, *Truth in History* (Cambridge: Belknap Press of Harvard University Press, 1979), 122, and C. L. Sonnichsen, *The Ambidextrous Historian* (Norman: University of Oklahoma Press, 1981), 12.

Chapter 9

1. A. Hunter Dupree, *Science in the Federal Government: A History of Policies and Activities to 1940* (Cambridge: Belknap Press of Harvard University Press, 1957; reprint with the addition of a twelve-page preface, Baltimore and London: Johns Hopkins University Press, 1986), 29.

2. Ibid., 139ff.

3. Committee on Scientific Surveys of the Territories of the United States, *Surveys of the Territories,* 45th Cong., 3d sess. (Serial 1861), 2.

4. Ibid., 2–5.

5. Doris Ostrander Dawdy, *Congress in Its Wisdom: The Bureau of Reclamation and the Public Interest* (Boulder, Col.: Westview Press, 1989), 9–10. The title of this book was suggested in part by the phrase uttered by Captain Hiram Chittenden's superior in the 1890s when Chittenden urged the corps to get more aggressively involved in irrigation studies, then underway. His superior's response was that he would "let Congress in its wisdom" decide.

6. *Congressional Record,* 45th Cong., 3d sess., February 11, 1879, 1203–4, 1207.

7. James H. Simpson, *Report of Explorations across the Great Basin of the Territory of Utah for a Direct Wagon-Route from Camp Floyd to Genoa, in Carson Valley, in 1859* (Washington, D.C.: Government Printing Office, 1876; reprint, Reno: University of Nevada Press, 1983).

8. Frank N. Schubert, *Vanguard of Expansion: Army Engineers in the Trans-Mississippi West, 1819–1879* (Washington, D.C.: Government Printing Office, 1987), 76, and David J. Weber, *Richard H. Kern: Expeditionary Artist in the Far Southwest, 1848–1853* (Albuquerque: University of New Mexico Press, 1985).

9. Thurman Wilkins, *Clarence King* (New York: Macmillan Company, 1958), 94.

10. William H. Goetzmann, *Exploration and Empire: The Explorer and Scientist in the Winning of the American West* (New York: Knopf, 1966), 309–11, 495, and Mary C. Rabbitt, *Minerals, Lands, and Geology for the Common Defense and General Welfare,* (Washington, D.C.: U.S. Geological Survey), 1:125–26.

11. Rabbitt, *Minerals, Lands, and Geology,* 209.

12. 15 U.S. Statutes, 306; Goetzmann, *Exploration and Empire,* 472, 496–98; and Committee on Public Lands, "Geographical and Geological Surveys West of the Mississippi, 43d Cong., 1st sess., H. Rept. 612 (Serial 1626), 31.

13. F. V. Hayden, *Preliminary Report of the United States Geological Survey of Wyoming* (Washington, D.C.: Government Printing Office, 1871), 7.

14. Dupree, *Science,* 210, and Clifford M. Nelson, Mary C. Rabbitt, and Fritiof M. Fryxell, "Ferdinand Vandeveer Hayden: The U.S. Geological Survey Years, 1879–1886," *Proceedings of the American Philosophical Society* 125, no. 3 (June 1981): 238–43.

15. Willie Arthur Chalfant, *Death Valley: The Facts* (Stanford, Cal.: Stanford University Press, 1930; reprint, 1953), 53; Executive Report of Lt. R. Birnie, Jr., Thirteenth United States Infantry, on the Operations of Party No. 2, California Section, Field Season of 1875, app. D, 130–35, in *Annual Report upon the Geographical Surveys West of the One Hundredth Meridian,* by George M. Wheeler, app. JJ of *Annual Report of the Chief of Engineers* (Washington, D.C.: Government Printing Office, 1876).

16. Eric Bergland, *Preliminary Report upon the Operations of Party No. 3, California Section, Season of 1875–76, with a View to Determine the Feasibility of Diverting the Colorado River for Purposes of Irrigation,* in Wheeler, *Annual Report* (1876), app. B, 109–19.

17. Richard A. Bartlett, *Great Surveys of the American West* (Norman: University of Oklahoma Press, 1962), 369; *Publications of the Geological Survey 1879–1961* (Washington, D.C.: Government Printing Office, 1962), 249–59.

18. F. V. Hayden, *United States Geological and Geographical Atlas of Colorado and Portions of Adjacent Territory,* U.S. Department of the Interior, 1877.

19. James T. Gardiner (or Gardner), "The Hayden Survey in Colorado in 1873 and 1874," with notes by Roger W. Toll, *The Colorado Magazine* 6, no. 4 (July 1929): 149.

20. Committee on Public Lands, 43d Cong., 1st sess., H. Rept. 612, 51–52, 57.

21. Russell R. Elliott, *Servant of Power* (Reno: University of Nevada Press, 1983), 112–18.

22. Dupree, *Science,* 232–35, and Dawdy, *Congress in Its Wisdom,* 8.

23. Dawdy, *Congress in Its Wisdom,* 8, and Elliott, *Servant of Power.*

24. Wheeler, *Irrigation in the United States of America,* (np.: np., 1892).

25. Dawdy, *Congress in Its Wisdom,* 9.

Chapter 10

1. George Crossette, *Founders of The Cosmos Club of Washington* (Washington, D.C.: Cosmos Club, 1966), 87–88.

2. Ibid., 154–56. Dwight L. Smith, "The Wheeler Survey in Utah, Idaho, and Montana: Samuel E. Tillman's Tour of Duty," *Utah Historical Quarterly* 59, no. 2 (Spring 1991): 146–63. *Who Was Who in American History: The Military* (Chicago: Marquis Who's Who, 1975); and *Who Was Who in America* (Chicago: Marquis Who's Who, 1967).

3. *Dictionary of American Biography* (New York: Charles Scribner's Sons, 1927–1964); *Who Was Who in America;* and George W. Cullum, *Biographical Register of the Officers and Graduates of the U.S. Military Academy at West Point* (Boston and New York: Houghton Mifflin and Company, 1891).

4. *Membership of the Cosmos Club* [1878–1968] (Washington, D.C.: Cosmos Club, 1968).

5. Thomas G. Manning, *Government in Science: The U.S. Geological Survey, 1867–1894* (Lexington: University of Kentucky Press, 1967), 95, 208ff.

6. Russell R. Elliott, *Servant of Power: A Political Biography of Senator William M. Stewart* (Reno: University of Nevada Press, 1983), 115–18.

7. Elbert B. Smith, *Francis Preston Blair* (New York: Macmillan Publishing Co., 1988). After Lucy's father James Blair died in 1853, Francis Blair provided a cottage on his estate at Silver Spring, Maryland, for James's widow and her two children. Lucy, the younger, was born the year her father died.

8. Emory to Editor, *New York Tribune,* June 12, 1874, 1332GR1874, Record Group 77, National Archives.

9. Simpson to Humphreys, June 30, 1876, 1938GR1876, Record Group 77, National Archives.

10. Committee on Public Lands, "Geographical and Geological Surveys West of the Mississippi, 43d Cong, 1st sess., H. Rept. 612 (Serial 1626), 70; G. K. Gilbert, *Report on the Geology of the Henry Mountains* (Washington, D.C.: Government Printing Office, 1877); and F. V. Hayden, *United States Geological and Geographical Atlas of Colorado and Portions of Adjacent Territory* (U.S. Department of the Interior, 1877).

11. Committee on Scientific Surveys of the Territories of the United States, *Survey of the Territories,* 45th Cong., 3d sess. (Serial 1861), 2.

12. *Record of the Officers of the Corps of Engineers from January 1, 1882, to December 31, 1888* (second book), U.S. Engineer Office, Record Group 77, National Archives.

13. *Record of the Officers,* and *Army and Navy Journal* (March 29, 1884), 707.

14. *Army and Navy Journal* (May 17, 1890), 715, and (December 5, 1891), 248.

15. *Army and Navy Journal* (February 8, 1902), 567. Peter L. Guth, "George Montague Wheeler: Last Army Explorer of the American West," (diss., U.S. Military Academy, 1975), 63 (on file, Historical Division, Office of the Chief of Engineers).

16. Guth, "George Montague Wheeler," 63. Guth, a geologist, has provided much new information, including that of Wheeler's last years, when Wheeler was "plagued with lawsuits" and "evictions for nonpayment of rent," in addition to illness and "many operations."

Selected Bibliography

Abbott, A. L. *Nevada Ghost Town Trails.* Anaheim, Cal.: Main Street Press, 1973.

Altshuler, Constance Wynn. *Chains of Command: Arizona and the Army, 1856–1875.* Tucson: Arizona Historical Society, 1981.

———. *Starting with Defiance: Nineteenth Century Arizona Military Posts.* Tucson: Arizona Historical Society, 1983.

Angel, Myron, ed. *History of Nevada.* Berkeley, Cal.: Howell-North, 1958 (reproduction of Thompson and West's *History of Nevada,* 1881, with introduction by David F. Myrick).

Ashbaugh, Don. *Nevada's Turbulent Yesterday.* Los Angeles: Westernlore Press, 1963.

Balch, William Ralston. *The Mines and Mining Interests of the United States in 1882.* Philadelphia: Mining Industrial Publishing House, 1882.

Barnes, Will C. *Arizona Place Names.* Tucson: University of Arizona, 1935 (rev. and enl. by Byrd H. Granger. Tucson: University of Arizona Press, 1960).

Bartlett, Richard A. *Great Surveys of the American West.* Norman: University of Oklahoma Press, 1962.

Beebe, Lucius, and Charles Clegg. *San Francisco's Golden Era: A Picture of San Francisco before the Fire.* Berkeley, Cal: Howell-North, 1960.

Bermingham, Peter. "Alexander H. Wyant: Some Letters from Abroad." *Archives of American Art Journal* (Smithsonian Institution) 12, no. 4 (1972).

———. *American Art in the Barbizon Mood.* Washington, D.C.: Smithsonian Institution Press, 1975.

Biographical Directory of the American Congress. Washington, D.C.: Government Printing Office, 1928.

Blair, Edward. *Leadville: Colorado's Magic City.* Boulder, Col.: Pruett Publishing Company, 1980.

Brandes, Ray. *Frontier Military Posts of Arizona.* Globe, Ariz.: Dale Stuart King, 1960.

Caffin, Charles H. "Alexander H. Wyant." Chap. 10 in *American Masters of Painting.* New York: Doubleday, Page & Company, 1906.

Carlson, Helen S. *Nevada Place Names: A Geographical Dictionary.* Reno: University of Nevada Press, 1974.

Casebier, Dennis G. *Camp Beale's Springs and the Hualpai Indians.* Norco, Cal.: Tales of the Mojave Road Publishing Company, 1980.

———. *Fort Pah-Ute, California.* Norco, Cal.: Tales of the Mojave Road Publishing Company, 1980.

———. *The Mojave Road.* Norco, Cal.: Tales of the Mojave Road Publishing Company, 1975.

Chalfant, Willie Arthur. *Death Valley: The Facts.* Stanford, Cal.: Stanford, London, Milford, Oxford, 1930. Reprint 1953.

______. *The Story of Inyo.* Rev. ed. Bishop, Cal.: n.p., 1933.

Clark, Eliot. *Alexander Wyant.* New York: n.p., 1916.

Corbett, Thomas B. *The Colorado Directory of Mines . . . and a History of Colorado.* Denver: Rocky Mountain News Printing Company, 1879.

Crampton, C. Gregory, and W. L. Rusho, "A Report on the History of Lee's Ferry, Arizona." Washington, D.C.: National Park Service, 1965. Mimeo.

Crossette, George. *Founders of the Cosmos Club of Washington.* Washington, D.C.: Cosmos Club, 1966.

Cullum, George W. *Biographical Register of the Officers and Graduates of the U.S. Military Academy at West Point.* Boston and New York: Houghton, Mifflin, and Company, 1891.

Current, Karen. *Photography and the Old West.* New York: Harry N. Abrams (in association with the Amon Carter Museum of Western Art), 1978.

Davis, William M. "Biographical Memoir of Grove Karl Gilbert." In *Memoirs, vol. 21.* Washington, D.C.: National Academy of Sciences, 1926.

Dawdy, Doris Ostrander. *Artists of the American West,* 3 vols. Athens: Swallow Press/Ohio University, 1987.

______. *Congress in Its Wisdom: The Bureau of Reclamation and the Public Interest.* Boulder, Col.: Westview Press, 1989.

______. "The Wyant Diary," *Arizona and the West* 22, no. 3 (Autumn 1980).

Degroot, Henry. "Silver Mines" (1860). Appendix to *First Directory of Nevada Territory.* Compiled by J. Wells Kelly. Los Gatos, Cal.: Talisman Press, 1962 (contains a "description of the Soil, Climate and Mineral Resources of the Country East of the Sierra").

Dellenbaugh, Frederick S. *A Canyon Voyage.* New York: G. P. Putnam's Sons, 1908. Reprint. Yale University Press, 1962.

Dewing, C. E., "The Wheeler Survey Records: A Study in Archival Anomaly" *The American Archivist* 27 (April 1964).

Dictionary of American Biography. New York: Charles Scribner's Sons, 1927–1964.

Dingus, Rick. *The Photographic Artifacts of Timothy O'Sullivan.* Albuquerque: University of New Mexico Press, 1982.

Dockstader, Frederick J. *The Kachina and the White Man.* Bloomfield Hills, Mich.: Cranbrook Institute of Science, 1954.

Dupree, A. Hunter. *Science in the Federal Government: A History of Policies and Activities to 1940.* Cambridge: Belknap Press of Harvard University Press, 1957; Baltimore and London: Johns Hopkins University Press, 1986.

Eberhart, Perry. *Guide to the Colorado Ghost Towns and Mining Camps.* Denver: Sage Books, 1929.

Elliott, Russell R. *Servant of Power: A Political Biography of Senator William M. Stewart.* Reno: University of Nevada Press, 1983.

Ewan, Joseph. *Rocky Mountain Naturalists.* Denver: University of Denver Press, 1950.

Federal Writers' Project. *Death Valley.* Boston: Houghton Mifflin Company, 1939.

———. *Idaho.* Caldwell, Idaho: Caxton Printers, 1938.

———. *Nevada.* Portland, Ore.: Binfords & Mort, 1940.

———. *Utah.* 2d ed. New York: Hastings House, 1945.

Fenton, Carroll Lane, and Mildred Adams Fenton. *Giants of Geology: The Story of the Great Geologists.* Garden City, N.J.: Doubleday, Doran & Co., 1945; enl. ed. Country Life Press, 1952.

Fossett, Frank. *Colorado, Its Gold and Silver Mines.* 2d ed. New York, 1879; Reprint. Glorieta, N.M.: Rio Grande Press, 1976.

Frazer, Robert W. *Forts of the West.* Norman: University of Oklahoma Press, 1965.

Gage, Eleanor Richardson. "Alexander H. Wyant: A Pioneer of American Landscape Painting." *Arts and Decoration* 2, no. 10 (August 1912).

Gardiner, James T. "The Hayden Survey in Colorado in 1873 and 1874," with notes by Roger W. Toll. *The Colorado Magazine* 6, no. 4 (July 1929).

Gilbert, Grove Karl. "Notes." Accessions 3372–3388. Records of the Geological Survey. Record Group 57, National Archives.

Goetzmann, William H. *Exploration and Empire: The Explorer and Scientist in the Winning of the American West.* New York: Alfred A. Knopf, 1966.

Granger , Byrd H., ed. *Will Barnes' Arizona Place Names.* Tucson: University of Arizona Press, 1960.

Grant, Bruce. *American Forts: Yesterday and Today.* New York: E. P. Dutton & Co., 1965.

Grant, Campbell. *Canyon de Chelly: Its People and Rock Art.* Tucson: University of Arizona Press, 1978.

Gregory, Herbert E. *The Navajo Country: A Geographic and Hydrographic Reconnaissance of Parts of Arizona, New Mexico, and Utah.* United States Geological Survey Water-Supply Paper 380. Washington, D.C.: Government Printing Office, 1916.

Gudde, Erwin G. *California Gold Camps.* Edited by Elisabeth K. Gudde. Berkeley: University of California Press, 1975.

———. *California Place Names.* Berkeley and Los Angeles: University of California Press, 1974.

Guth, Peter L., "George Montague Wheeler: Last Army Explorer of the American West." Diss., U.S. Military Academy, 1975. Historical Division, Office of the Chief of Engineers, Washington, D.C.

Hack, John T. *The Changing Physical Environment of the Hopi Indians of Arizona.* Cambridge: Peabody Museum of American Archaeology and Ethnology, Harvard University, 1942.

Haines, Aubrey L. *Yellowstone National Park: Its Exploration and Establishment.* Washington, D.C.: U.S. Department of the Interior, National Park Service, 1974.

Harris, Beth Kay. *The Towns of Tintic.* Denver: Sage Books, 1961.

Hayden, F. V. *Preliminary Report of the United States Geological Survey of Wyoming and Portions of Contiguous Territories.* Washington, D.C.: n.p., 1871.

———. *United States Geological and Geographical Atlas of Colorado and Portions of Adjacent Territory.* U.S. Department of the Interior, 1877.

Heitmann, Francis B. *Historical Register and Dictionary of the United States Army,* vol. 1. Washington, D.C.: Government Printing Office, 1903.

Hine, Robert V. *Edward Kern and American Expansion.* New Haven and London: Yale University Press, 1972.

Hualapai Tribe of the Hualapai Reservation, Arizona, v. *United States of America.* Docket No. 90, Indian Claims Commission.

Ives, Joseph C. *Report upon the Colorado River of the West.* 36th Cong., 1st sess., H. Doc. 90. Washington, D.C.: Government Printing Office, 1861.

Jenkinson, Michael. *Ghost Towns of New Mexico: Playthings in the Wind.* Albuquerque: University of New Mexico Press, 1967.

Jones, Fayette A. *Old Mining Camps of New Mexico, 1854–1904.* Santa Fe, N.M.; Stagecoach Press, 1964.

Kessell, John L. *Kiva, Cross, and Crown: The Pecos Indians and New Mexico, 1540–1840.* Washington, D.C.: National Park Service, U.S. Department of the Interior, 1979.

King, David S. *Mountain Meadows Massacre: A Search for Perspective.* Washington, D.C.: Potomac Corral of the Westerners, 1970.

Leigh, Rufus Wood. *Five Hundred Utah Place Names: Their Origin and Significance.* Salt Lake City: Deseret News Press, 1961.

———. *Nevada Place Names: Their Origin and Significance.* Boulder City, Nev.: Lake Mead Natural History Association, 1964.

Malach, Roman. *Peach Springs in Mohave County.* Kingman: Arizona Bicentennial Commission, 1975.

Manning, Thomas G. *Government in Science: The U.S. Geological Survey, 1867–1894.* Lexington: University of Kentucky Press, 1967.

Mariger, Marietta M. *Saga of Three Towns: Harrisburg, Leeds, Silver Reef.* Panguitch, Utah: Garfield County News, n.d.

Measeles, Evelyn Brack. *Lee's Ferry.* Boulder, Col.: Pruett Publishing Company, 1981.

Meisel, Max. *A Bibliography of American Natural History.* 3 vols. Brooklyn, N.Y.: Premier Publishing Co., 1924.

Mining Directory of San Miguel, Ouray, San Juan and La Plata Counties. Denver: County Directory Company, 1899.

Montgomery, Walter, "Alexander H. Wyant," in *American Art and American Art Collections.* New York and London: Garland Publishing, 1978.

Moore, Richard T., and Eldred D. Wilson. *Bibliography of the Geology and Mineral Resources of Arizona, 1848–1964.* Tucson: University of Arizona Press, 1965.

Murbarger, Nell. *Ghosts of the Adobe Walls: Human Interest and Historical Highlights from 400 Ghost Haunts of Old Arizona.* Los Angeles: Westernlore Press, 1969.

Murphy, Lawrence R. *Frontier Crusader William F. M. Arny.* Tucson: University of Arizona Press, 1972.

National Cyclopaedia of American Biography. New York: James T. White & Company, 1893–1969.

Nelson, Clifford M., Mary C. Rabbitt, and Fritiof M. Fryxell. "Ferdinand Vandeveer Hayden: The U.S. Geological Survey Years, 1879–1886" in *Proceedings of the American Philosophical Society* 125, no. 3 (June 1981).

Nevada: The Silver State. 2 vols. Carson City, Nev.: Western States Historical Publishers, 1970.

Olpin, Robert S. *Alexander Helwig Wyant, 1836–1892.* (Salt Lake City: Utah Museum of Fine Arts, 1968 (catalog, essay, and chronology).

Ostrander, Gilman M. *Nevada: The Great Rotten Borough, 1859–1964.* New York: Alfred A. Knopf, 1966.

Paher, Stanley W. *Nevada Ghost Towns and Mining Camps*. Berkeley, Cal.: Howell-North Books, 1970.

Paul, Rodman W. *California Gold: The Beginning of Mining in the Far West*. Lincoln and London: University of Nebraska Press, 1965.

———. *Mining Frontiers of the Far West, 1848–1880*. New York: Holt, Rinehart and Winston, 1963.

Pearce, Thomas Matthews. *New Mexico Place Names*. Albuquerque: University of New Mexico Press, 1965.

Peterson, Charles S. *Take Up Your Mission: Mormon Colonizing along the Little Colorado, 1870–1900*. Tucson: University of Arizona Press, 1973.

———. *Utah: A Bicentennial History*. New York: W. W. Norton & Company, 1977.

Powell, John Wesley. *Report on the Lands of the Arid Region of the United States*. 2d ed. Washington, D.C.: Government Printing Office, 1879.

Powell, William H. *Powell's Records of Living Officers of the United States Army*. Philadelphia: L. R. Hamersly & Co., 1890.

Prucha, Francis Paul. *A Guide to the Military Posts of the United States, 1789–1895*. Madison: State Historical Society of Wisconsin, 1964.

Pyne, Stephen J. *Grove Karl Gilbert: A Great Engine of Research*. Austin: University of Texas Press, 1980.

Rabbitt, Mary C. *Minerals, Lands, and Geology for the Common Defence and General Welfare*. 3 vols. Washington, D.C.: U.S. Geological Survey, 1879–1986.

Raymond, Rossiter W. *Statistics of Mines and Mining in the States and Territories West of the Rocky Mountains*. 8 vols. Washington, D.C.: Government Printing Office, 1869–1877.

Rummell, John, and E. M. Berlin, "The Genius of Wyant." In *Aims and Ideals of Representative American Painters*. Buffalo, N.Y.: n.p., 1901.

Rusho, W. L., and C. Gregory Crampton. *Desert River Crossing: Historic Lee's Ferry on the Colorado River*. Santa Barbara, Cal., and Salt Lake City: Peregrine Smith, 1981.

Schubert, Frank N. *Vanguard of Expansion: Army Engineers in the Trans-Mississippi West, 1819–1879*. Washington, D.C.: Government Printing Office, 1987.

Shenon, Philip J., and Roy P. Full. *An Evaluation Study of the Mineral Resources in the Lands of the Hualapai Tribe of Indians of Arizona as Decided on November 19, 1962 before the Indian Claims Commission*. 4 vols. Salt Lake City: n.p., 1964.

Sherman, James, and Barbara H. Sherman. *Ghost Towns of Arizona.* Norman: University of Oklahoma Press, 1969.

Smith, Dwight L. "Hoskaninni: A Gold Mining Venture in Glen Canyon." In *Probing the American West,* edited by K. Ross Toole and others. Santa Fe: Museum of New Mexico Press, 1962.

Smith, Dwight L., and C. Gregory Crampton, eds. *The Colorado River Survey: Robert B. Stanton and the Denver, Colorado Canyon and Pacific Railroad.* Salt Lake City and Chicago: Howe Brothers, 1987.

Stegner, Wallace. *Mormon Country.* New York: Duell, Sloan & Pearce, 1942.

———. *The Sound of Mountain Water.* Garden City, N.J.: Doubleday & Company, 1969.

Taylor, Morris F. *First Mail West: Stagecoach Lines on the Santa Fe Trail.* Albuquerque: University of New Mexico Press, 1971.

Taylor, Ralph C. *Colorado: South of the Border.* Denver: Sage Books, 1963.

U.S. Department of Defense. *Glossary of Mapping, Charting, and Geodetic Terms.* 2d ed. Washington, D.C., 1969.

U.S. Department of the Interior, U.S. Geological Survey. *John Wesley Powell: Soldier, Explorer, Scientist.* Washington, D.C.: Government Printing Office, 1970.

Van Dyke, John C. "Alexander H. Wyant." Chap. 3 in *American Painting and Its Tradition.* New York: Charles Scribner's Sons, 1919.

Walker, Henry P., and Don Bufkin. *Historical Atlas of Arizona.* Norman: University of Oklahoma Press, 1979.

Weber, David J. *Richard H. Kern: Expeditionary Artist in the Far Southwest, 1848–1853.* Albuquerque: University of New Mexico Press, 1985.

Webster's American Military Biographies. Springfield, Mass.: G. and C. Merriam Company, 1978.

Wheeler, George M. *Preliminary Report upon a Reconnaissance through Southern and Southeastern Nevada, Made in 1869.* Rev. ed. of the 1870 report. Washington, D.C.: Government Printing Office, 1875.

———. *Preliminary Report of Explorations in Nevada and Arizona.* Washington, D.C.: Government Printing Office, 1872. Also published in *Annual Report of the Chief of Engineers.* 42d Cong., 2d sess. S. Doc. 65. Serial 1479.

———. *Progress Report upon Geographical and Geological Explorations and Surveys West of the One Hundredth Meridian in 1872.* Washington, D.C.: Government Printing Office, 1874.

———. *Annual Report upon the Geographical Explorations and Surveys West of the One Hundredth Meridian.* Washington, D.C.: Government Printing Office, 1874. Also published in *Annual Report of the Chief of Engineers.* 43d Cong., 2d sess. H. Doc. 1, pt. 2. Serial 1637.

———. *Annual Report upon the Geographical Explorations and Surveys West of the One Hundredth Meridian.* Washington, D.C.: Government Printing Office, 1875. Also published in *Annual Report of the Chief of Engineers.* H. 44th Cong., 1st sess. Doc. 1, pt. 2, vol. 2. Serial 1676.

———. *Annual Report upon the Geographical Explorations and Surveys West of the One Hundredth Meridian.* Washington, D.C.: Government Printing

Office, 1876. Also published in *Annual Report of the Chief of Engineers.* 44th Cong., 2d sess. H. Doc. 1, pt. 2, vol. 2, pt. 3. Serial 1745.

———. *Annual Report upon the Geographical Explorations and Surveys West of the One Hundredth Meridian.* Washington, D.C: Government Printing Office, 1877. Also published in *Annual Report of the Chief of Engineers.* 45th Cong., 2d sess. H. Doc. 1, pt. 2, vol. 2, pt. 2. Serial 1796.

———. *Annual Report upon the Geographical Explorations and Surveys West of the One Hundredth Meridian.* Washington, D.C.: Government Printing Office, 1878. Also published in *Annual Report of the Chief of Engineers.* 45th Cong., 3d sess. H. Doc 1, pt. 2, vol. 2, pt. 3. Serial 1846.

———. *Annual Report upon the Geographical Explorations and Surveys West of the One Hundredth Meridian.* Washington, D.C.: Government Printing Office, 1879. Also published in *Annual Report of the Chief of Engineers.* 46th Cong., 2d sess. H. Doc. 1, pt. 2, vol. 2, pt. 3. Serial 1906.

———. "Facts Regarding the Government Land and Marine Surveys of the United States." Extract from *Report on the Third International Geographical Congress.* Washington, D.C.: Government Printing Office, 1885. This also appears in Wheeler's *Final Report,* vol. 1, 1889, pp. 415–79.

———. *Report upon United States Geographical Surveys West of the One Hundredth Meridian.* 7 vols. (vol. 1 written by Wheeler). Washington, D.C.: Government Printing Office, 1889.

———. "Irrigation in the United States of America." Privately printed, 1892 (16 pp.).

Wheeler, George M. (assisted by D. W. Lockwood). *Preliminary Report of the General Features Of the Military Reconnaissance* [sic] *through Southern Nevada . . . , 1869.* San Francisco: n.p., 1870.

Who Was Who in American History: The Military. Chicago: Marquis Who's Who, 1975.

Wilkins, Thurman. *Clarence King: A Biography.* New York: Macmillan Company, 1958.

Wilson, Neill C. *Silver Stampede: The Career of Death Valley's Hell-Camp, Old Panamint.* New York: Macmillan Company, 1937.

Wolle, Muriel Sibell. *Stampede to Timberline: The Ghost Towns and Mining Camps of Colorado.* Boulder, Col.: Muriel S. Wolle, 1949.

Index

A Note about the Author

Doris Dawdy has been a free-lance writer specializing in Western subjects since 1960. She is currently working on a book on trends in water management in the West, highlighting the effect of litigation during the early years of Western development.